THE INSIDE STORY

Have *you* heard what **JESUS** is saying about *YOU?*

THE INSIDE STORY

Have *you* heard what **JESUS** is saying about *YOU?*

Connie **WITTER**
Rose **KARLEBACH**
& Kelly **RAY**

because of Jesus publishing

The Inside Story
Have You Heard What Jesus is Saying About You?

ISBN: 0-9779972-3-5
Copyright © 2009 by *Because of Jesus Publishing*

BECAUSE OF JESUS PUBLISHING
P.O. Box 3064
Broken Arrow, OK 74013

Cover design and Layout: Nan Bishop, Tulsa, Oklahoma
nbishopsdesigns@cox.net
Edited by Rose Karlebach, Tulsa, Oklahoma
onlyroseofsharon@gmail.com

TABLE OF CONTENTS

Foreword 9

Introduction 10

WEEK 1 **TRADING PLACES**

You're a Princess Because of Jesus — Connie Witter 13

   Day 1 I Am a Princess 14

   Day 2 I Am Righteous 20

   Day 3 I Am Destined to Reign 26

WEEK 2 **THE FEARLESS FACTOR**

You're Loved By Jesus — Connie Witter 33

   Day 1 I Am Loved 34

   Day 2 I Am Aware of the Enemy's Lies 40

   Day 3 I Agree with Jesus 45

WEEK 3 **ARE YOU SMARTER THAN A FIFTH GRADER?**

You're Wise Because of Jesus — Kelly Ray 53

   Day 1 I Am Wise 54

   Day 2 I Am Led by God's Spirit 60

   Day 3 I Am Confident 66

WEEK 4 **AMERICA'S NEXT TOP MODEL**

You're Beautiful Because of Jesus — Kelly Ray 73

   Day 1 I Am Beautiful 74

   Day 2 I Am Perfect 80

   Day 3 I Am Beautiful Within 85

WEEK 5 **THE COMPARISON TRAP**

You're Valuable Because of Jesus — Connie Witter 91

    Day 1 I Am Valuable 92

    Day 2 I Am Special.. 98

    Day 3 I Am Worthy of Love.. 102

    Day 4 I Am Worth the Wait 107

WEEK 6 **BEST FRIENDS FOREVER**

You're Accepted Because of Jesus — Connie Witter.................... 112

    Day 1 I Am Accepted 114

    Day 2 I Am Approved 119

    Day 3 I Am Favored 124

WEEK 7 **AMERICAN IDOL**

You're Wonderful Because of Jesus — Rose Karlebach 131

    Day 1 I Am Wonderful.. 132

    Day 2 I Am Adored 137

    Day 3 I Am Gifted... 142

WEEK 8 **EXTREME MAKEOVER**

You're Loving Because of Jesus — Rose Karlebach 149

    Day 1 I Am a Loving 150

    Day 2 I Am a Forgiving.. 156

    Day 3 I Am An Encourager.. 162

DEDICATION

Connie This book is lovingly dedicated to my wonderful Savior, Jesus. Your love for me has truly made my heart whole. Thank you for making me a genuine princess in your Kingdom. My greatest desire is to bring glory to your name. I would also like to dedicate this book to the special princesses in my life whom I love so very much: my two beautiful daughters, Kristen and Victoria Witter, and three wonderful nieces, Rachel, Olivia, and Amanda Rose. Thank you for helping me write this devotional by reading through the manuscript and sharing your heart with me. And to my wonderful daughter-in-law, Jessica, and granddaughter, Ryann, I'm so glad God brought you both into my life to love. And to my two youngest nieces, Briona and Brooklyn Beckham. My greatest desire for each of you is that you would realize who you truly are in Jesus and live confident and secure in His love.

Kelly I would like to dedicate this book to my daughter, Elizabeth and her first Bible study group: Courtney, Holland, Meg, Sara, Kennedy, Christina, Lexi, Jessica, and Emily. They were the examples Jesus used to motivate me to press forward and write this book, so that many more girls could know how Jesus sees them. I would like to thank my loving husband Mark who was so supportive and helpful. I would also like to thank Connie, Rose and Regina for doing this together with me. Most of all I would like to thank my King, Jesus, for showing me it's never too late to be a princess and live happily-ever-after.

Rose This book has been a labor of love, dedicated to my wonderful Savior, Jesus, and my patient, loving and very funny husband Paul, as well as all the girls in my life who have been a source of inspiration. First of all, I want to thank all of my wonderful Bible Study friends without whose faithfulness this book would never have been written — you know who you are! I especially want to thank Connie for being such a wonderful mentor and encourager; Kelly, for hearing from the Holy Spirit and inspiring us to write this book, and Nancy Bishop, whose artistry has made our words look amazing on the printed page. Secondly, I want to thank my very first "girl" friends: my mom, Geri and wonderful sisters, Phyllis, Nan and Billie who have always loved me unconditionally. And it goes without saying that I could not have written it without having experienced the love of my two beautiful daughters, Jasmine and Ariel. My prayer is that this book will be a source of encouragement to them, their friends, and every girl, no matter what age, who opens it.

FOREWORD

The *Inside Story: Have You Heard What Jesus is Saying About You?* was lovingly and thoughtfully created by us and is dedicated to each of our daughters, their friends and other young women, so that they might experience the same victories we have as a result of the *Because of Jesus Bible Study*. Our hope is that as they go through it, they will learn as we have, to have an abiding relationship with Jesus and to walk in the freedom and abundant life He purchased for us. Through this simple 8-Week Devotional for young girls, our desire is that they will come to know just how valuable and precious they are to God, to recognize and receive the truths which Jesus says about them, and to identify and reject the lies that the enemy tries to get them to believe. Our desire is that at the end of this study, they would have a deeper understanding of what Jesus has done for them and who He has made them to be: a princess in the kingdom of God.

As we put this devotional together, we created it to appeal to girls of varying ages and from different backgrounds. We realize, however, that during the course of their study, there may be some girls who have never entered into a relationship with Jesus. For this purpose we have also included this simple prayer to help them begin their journey:

Dear Jesus: Thank You so much for dying on the cross for me, paying for my sins, taking on the punishment that I deserved and giving me the righteousness that only You deserved. You are the Author and Finisher of my faith, Jesus. Help me to learn what You say about me, and to distinguish between the truth of what You say and the lies of the enemy. Help me to always look to You for the power (grace) to walk in the truth that You show me and to cast down the enemy's lies. Thank You, that as I study your Word, I will see more and more who I am in You and to You: a princess in your kingdom.

INTRODUCTION

In a world where beauty, acceptance, and approval are highly sought after, girls, beginning at a very young age, find themselves measuring their worth by the world's unattainable standards. Critical, negative thoughts like, *She's prettier than me; They don't like me; I have to perform well to gain their approval; I don't fit in; I must not be good enough,* and others bombard them on a daily basis, causing them to experience rejection and disapproval in their tender hearts, and to believe that they won't ever measure up no matter how hard they try. These same negative thoughts are common to all of us, and actually had their beginning a long time ago, in the garden of Eden.

In the beginning, Adam and Eve were made in God's image: perfect, accepted, loved and adored by their Heavenly Father. All of their physical and emotional needs were met; they lacked nothing. Their hearts were happy and their lives were complete in relationship with their Heavenly Father and with each other. The Father gave them his stamp of approval; He called them *good*.

But Adam and Eve had an enemy, the devil, who wanted to create a separation between them and their loving Heavenly Father. He devised a subtle plan to get Eve to question the truth about what God had actually said about her. Through his lies he convinced her that she and Adam were incomplete; that something was missing from their lives and that they weren't quite good enough. Because Eve bought into the devil's negative lies by believing them, it created a separation between her and her Heavenly Father. As a result, sadness entered her heart, and from then on, into the heart of every person who would ever be born upon the earth.

Although that took place a long time ago, the devil is still trying to bring his same plan to pass in young girls' lives today, by lying to them the same way he did to Eve, hoping they will believe his lies instead of God's truth. *There is something wrong with you,* he whispers in their impressionable ears. *You're not perfect enough; You don't measure up; You're not valuable, wonderful, or accepted.* Through his lies he brings sadness into their hearts, which creates insecurity, fear, and lack of confidence as a result of not knowing the truth.

But thank goodness, God loved us so much that He didn't leave us in that sad state, but created a plan through Jesus, to restore us back into perfect relationship with the Father. Jesus came and died on the cross for our sins, making a way for us to be perfect, approved and accepted by God once again. He came to tell us that we are beautiful, valuable, accepted, wonderful, and perfect in every way, and that He thoroughly approves of us.

As each of you take this journey through the Bible with us, our prayer is that you will come to know the love of Jesus in a deeper way and begin to see yourselves the way He sees you. You'll begin to recognize the devil's lies and the negative feelings that come with them, and you'll replace those lies with the truth of God's word. You'll be changed from the inside out, as you discover your true identity and value in Jesus. We pray that you'll realize that no matter what age, you are a genuine princess and you're loved by the Prince of Peace. You are righteous, beautiful, valuable, accepted, and perfect in every way — because of Jesus!

because of Jesus

WEEK 1

TRADING PLACES

You're a Princess Because of Jesus

Connie Witter

Day 1
I Am a Princess

Day 2
I Am Righteous

Day 3
I Am Destined to Reign

Day 1
I Am a Princess

For He foreordained us (destined us, planned in love for us) to be adopted...as His own children through Jesus Christ.
—*Ephesians 1:5* AMP

God loved you so much that His plan from the beginning was to adopt you as His very own daughter through your faith in Jesus. An adopted child is special because she is handpicked and truly wanted by her parents. You, too, were handpicked by your Heavenly Father because He wanted you to be a part of His family. Not only that, when He adopted you to be His special daughter, you became a princess in His kingdom! **1 Peter 2:9** also tells us this same thing: *But you are a chosen race, a royal priesthood, a dedicated nation, [God's] own purchased, special people, that you may set forth the wonderful deeds and display the virtues and perfections of Him Who called you out of darkness into His marvelous light.* AMP

So, what makes a girl a princess? A girl is a princess because she's the daughter of a king. Since your Heavenly Father is the King of kings that means that you're a genuine princess!

As a young girl, I loved to watch princess movies like *Cinderella* and *Snow White*. I dreamed of what it would be like to be a princess. Even now as a grown woman I still love to watch movies about a prince and a princess falling in love. I so admire the qualities of a princess; she is beautiful, kind, and loving to those around her. She is special, adored, and deeply loved by her prince. Then I realized that because of Jesus, I am a princess!

Just like Cinderella and Snow White, your life is also a princess story, for not only are you the daughter of the King, you're also the bride of a Prince. In **John 15:16** Jesus spoke these words of comfort to you, *"You didn't choose me, I chose you"*, and In **Isaiah 54:5,** *"I made you. I am now your husband. My name is The Lord Who Rules Over All."* NIrV Jesus is the Prince of peace and He has chosen you to be his bride!

But even though princess stories are wonderful, you'll notice that in each one of them there is an evil person who speaks lies to the princess to keep her from fulfilling her destiny; for Cinderella, it was her wicked stepmother, for Snow White, the evil queen. And just like in every princess story, there is an evil person in your life who is constantly speaking lies to your heart. He is your enemy, the devil, and in **John 8:44** is actually called *"the father of lies."*AMP So, what kind of lies has he spoken to you? Perhaps you've heard him whisper these thoughts to your mind:

You're nobody special

You're not good enough

You don't belong

Thank goodness, that just like Snow White and Cinderella were ultimately rescued by the handsome prince who came to tell them how beautiful and loved they were, you too have a Prince who came to rescue you from the devil's lies. He came to set your heart free with His love.

Colossians 1:12-14 says, ...*always thanking the Father....For he has rescued us from the one who rules in the kingdom of darkness, and he has brought us into the Kingdom of his dear Son. God has purchased our freedom with his blood and has forgiven all our sins.* NLT All of us, at one time, lived in the kingdom of darkness. The Bible says we were sinners; our sins separated us from God and we were not a part of God's family (Ephesians 2:11-13). The Good News is that Jesus loved you so much that He came as your Prince, died for your sins and rescued you from the kingdom of darkness. When you put your trust in Him, all of your sins were forgiven and your identity was changed. You are now a princess in the kingdom of God and you don't have to listen to or believe the lies of the devil anymore. You now have the power to believe what Jesus says about you and live securely in His love.

Jesus, your Prince, always speaks the truth to your heart. This is what He has to say about you . . .

When I began to learn what Jesus had done for me and that I really am a princess in the kingdom of God, I began seeing myself in a different way. I realized that I am adored, valuable, and special because I truly am a daughter of the King of kings. Because of Jesus, I am everything I ever wanted to be. Instead of being insecure and worried about what other people thought of me and feeling like I didn't belong, I began to realize who I truly am in Jesus and it healed my heart and made me confident in His great love.

I chose you to be My princess.
John 15:16

Your sins are all forgiven.
You are perfect in My eyes.
Colossians 1:14, Hebrews 10:14

I love you. You belong to Me.
Ephesians 2:11-13

And the exact same thing is true of you. You don't have to wish you were a princess; you already are one! Jesus made you a princess when He died for you and chose you to be His bride. In his eyes you truly are beautiful, valuable and perfect in every way. His dream for you is that you see yourself the same way that He does.

So agree with what Jesus says about you. Speak the truth out loud:

♥ **I am a princess because of Jesus**

♥ **My sins are forgiven; I am perfect in my Father's eyes**

♥ **I belong to Jesus; I am loved by the King**

PRAYER: *Heavenly Father, I know You love me because You sent Jesus to rescue me from the kingdom of darkness and bring me into Your wonderful kingdom. Help me to see myself the way You do. I believe You when You say that I am special, important and deeply loved by You. And because of You, Jesus, I truly am a princess!*

STUDY QUESTIONS

Have you ever heard the devil speak these lies to your heart?

LIES EXPOSED

You're nobody special	_____ Yes	_____ No
You're not good enough	_____ Yes	_____ No
You don't belong	_____ Yes	_____ No

In **John 8:44** the devil is called *"the father of lies."* Why do you think the devil wants you to believe his lies?

_____

_____

NOW LET'S STUDY THE TRUTH TOGETHER

Read **Ephesians 1:5:** *For He foreordained us (destined us, planned in love for us) to be adopted as His own children through Jesus Christ.* AMP
In **Isaiah 54:4** Jesus said, *"I made you. I am now your Husband. I am the Lord Who rules over all."* NIrV
A princess is the daughter of a king or the bride of a prince. According to these verses, why are you a princess in the kingdom of God?

_____

_____

Read **Colossians 1:12-14**...*always thanking the Father.... For he has rescued us from the one who rules in the kingdom of darkness, and he has brought us into the Kingdom of His dear Son. God has purchased our freedom with his blood and has forgiven all our sins.* NLT
Your life truly is a princess story; you're a princess and Jesus is your Prince. According to these verses, explain what He did for you:

_____

_____

When you think of a princess, what do you see? Think of five words that describe a princess:

_____, _____, _____,

_____, and _____ .

Now that you've come to realize that you truly are a genuine princess, the five words you wrote down are really describing you. Fill in the blanks below with the words you used to describe a princess:

I am a princess in the kingdom of God. I am _____,
_____, _____, _____, and
_____ **because of Jesus!**

Write **T** next to the statements that are true and **L** next to the statements that are lies:
_____ I am a princess because of Jesus
_____ I'm not good enough to be a princess
_____ I'm nobody special
_____ My sins are forgiven and I'm perfect in my Father's eyes
_____ I don't belong
_____ I belong to Jesus and I am loved by the King

GOING DEEPER

TRUTH: **I am a princess in God's Kingdom**

Read **1 Peter 2:9** in your own Bible.
How will you see yourself differently now that you realize that you truly are royalty, a princess in God's kingdom?

_____

_____

Read **John 15:16.**
What did Jesus say to you in this verse? How does it make your heart feel to know that He has chosen you to be His bride?

_____

_____

JOURNAL ENTRY

Write a prayer to God. Talk to Him about the truth He showed you today:

_____

_____

_____

_____

_____

What is the main truth that you learned from today's devotion?

_____

_____

_____

_____

_____

you are a princess

Day 2
I Am Righteous

*I am overwhelmed with joy in the L*ORD *my God! For he has dressed me with the clothing of salvation, and draped me in a robe of righteousness. I am like…a bride with her jewels.* —Isaiah 61:10

*W*hen you put your faith in Jesus, and accepted His proposal to be His bride, He dressed you in a beautiful white robe of righteousness. Just like a bride changes her identity by changing her last name to her husband's name, Jesus changed your identity from who you used to be — a sinner — into his identity — a righteous princess in the kingdom of God. He is your prince charming; when He looks at you he sees a perfect, beautiful bride on her wedding day, and His good opinion of you will never change. You're a righteous princess because of His blood.

Romans 5:8-9 says, *But God proves His own love for us in that while we were still sinners, Christ died for us! … We have now been declared righteous by His blood.* HCSB

So, what does it mean to be declared *righteous* by His blood? The definition of the word *righteous* means "to conform to God's commands; to be good; justified and perfect in God's sight."[1]

In spite of this, we all know that there are times in our lives when we have not obeyed God's commands and have not treated others with love and kindness. We often fail to do what's right; to be good and act the way God would want us to.

Jesus was the only person who was truly righteous because He obeyed God's commands perfectly. Because of His great love for you, even though Jesus did nothing wrong, He was willing to trade places with you, take the blame for your sins and give you His righteousness as a gift of His love. You now have His nature. Your true identity is found in Him.

2 Corinthians 5:21 says, *Christ did no wrong thing. But for our sake God put the blame for our wrong ways on Christ. <u>So now God sees us as</u>*

<u>good</u>, because we are in Christ. WE

God wants you to stop trying and begin trusting. No matter how hard you try to be righteous by obeying God's commands, you can never be good enough in your own ability. So, Jesus did it for you. Simply by trusting Him, all your sins were wiped away with His blood. Now the Father sees you as good and righteous because you are in Jesus. The Bible says that Jesus made you perfect forever in the Father's eyes. (Hebrews 10:14).

I grew up in a Christian home and I tried so hard to be good, but somehow I always seemed to mess up. The temptations were always greater than my ability to resist. I remember one time in particular I got really angry with my sister. I yelled at her and told her everything that was wrong with her. Deep down, I was jealous of her, and thought she was much better than me. So I pointed out the things that were wrong with her in order to make myself feel better. Yet, after the fighting ended, I was left feeling bad about myself once again. I really wanted to be like Jesus, but because I often failed, I believed that I just wasn't good enough. To make matters worse, the devil would be right there when I failed, planting these negative lies in my mind:

> You're not **like** Jesus
>
> You **need** to try **harder** to **be** good
>
> You'll **never be** good **enough**

Then I began to really understand the truth of what Jesus had done for me. Listen to His words of love that He speaks to all of our hearts . . .

As I began thinking upon what Jesus said about me, my heart was set free from believing the lies of the enemy. I didn't have to try anymore in my own strength to be good enough; I could trust what

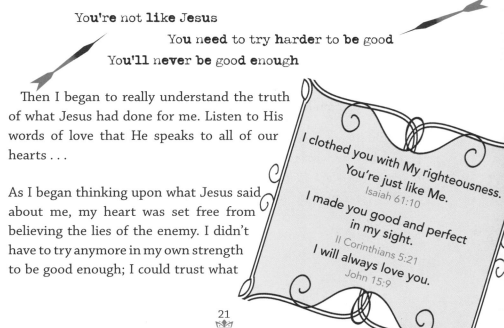

I clothed you with My righteousness. You're just like Me.
Isaiah 61:10

I made you good and perfect in my sight.
II Corinthians 5:21

I will always love you.
John 15:9

Jesus did for me and receive the truth: that I am already righteous and good because of Him. And it wasn't until I was an adult that I really began to believe who I am in Jesus. When I did, the jealousy I felt all my life toward my sister disappeared effortlessly. I realized we were both righteous and good in God's sight because of Jesus, and because of that, there was no need for me to be jealous anymore. As I agreed with His words of love toward me, Jesus gave me the power to begin loving my sister in the same way that He loved me.

The Good News is that you don't have to try anymore in your own strength to be good enough, either. Jesus clothed you with His righteousness; it's His wedding gift to you, His princess. Now that He has declared you righteous and good, you can agree with the truth that you already are just like Him. As you believe who you are in Jesus, His love will melt away any negative feelings you may feel toward someone else. His power will work in you to help you act more and more like the righteous princess He has declared you to be.

So agree with Jesus, the One Who loves you. Speak the truth out loud:

♥ **Jesus clothed me with His righteousness; I am just like Him**

♥ **I am good and perfect in my Father's eyes because of Jesus**

♥ **I am loved by the King**

PRAYER: *Thank You, Jesus. I know You love me because You took the punishment for my sins and clothed me with Your righteousness. Help me to remember who I am in You; that I am no longer a sinner, but righteous like You are. You made me good and perfect in my Father's eyes. I am just like You. I thank You that I do not have to be good in my own ability, but when I look to You for strength, You will help me to act just like You.*

STUDY QUESTIONS

Have you ever heard the devil speak these lies to your heart:

LIES EXPOSED

You're not **like** Jesus   _____ Yes _____ No

You need to try **harder**
to **be** good   _____ Yes _____ No

You'll ne**ver be** good eno**ugh**   _____ Yes _____ No

NOW LET'S STUDY THE TRUTH TOGETHER

Read **Isaiah 61:10:** *I am overwhelmed with joy in the* LORD *my God! For he has dressed me with the clothing of salvation and draped me in a robe of righteousness. I am like . . . a bride with her jewels.*

When Jesus asked you to be His princess and you accepted His invitation, what two things did He dress you in according to **Isaiah 61:10**?

_____

_____

Read **Romans 5:8-9:** *[8] But God proves His own love for us in that while we were still sinners Christ died for us! [9] ... we have now been declared righteous by His blood....* HCSB

How did God prove His love for you? (verse 8)

_____

What has God declared about you? (verse 9)

_____

You learned the definition of *righteous* in today's devotion. Put your name in the blank below and say this truth to yourself:

Because of the blood of Jesus, I, _____ am justified, good and perfect forever in my Father's eyes.

Read **2 Corinthians 5:21:** *Christ did no wrong thing. But for our sake God put the blame for our wrong ways on Christ. So now God sees us as good, because we are in Christ.* WE

Personalize this verse. Put your name in the blanks:

Christ did no wrong thing. But for _____'s sake God put the blame for _____'s wrong ways on Christ. So now God sees _____ as good, because I am in Christ.

Write **T** next to the statements that are true and **L** next to the statements that are lies:

_____ I'll never be good enough; I'll never be like Jesus
_____ I need to try harder to be good
_____ God sees me as good and perfect because of Jesus
_____ I am loved by the King
_____ I am righteous because of Jesus; I am just like Him

GOING DEEPER

TRUTH: Jesus traded places with me; I am righteous because of Him

Read **Hebrews 10:14** in your own Bible.

Write your name in the blank below:

By offering Himself as a sacrifice for my sins, Jesus made _____ perfect forever in God's sight.

Jesus made you good and perfect in God's sight. How does it make you feel to know that Jesus traded places with you by taking the punishment for your sins and giving you His righteousness?

_____

_____

_____

In today's devotion, we learned that God wants you to stop trying to be good and begin to trust that you are already good in His sight because of Jesus. Why do you think that believing that you are already righteous and good in Him empowers you to treat others with love and kindness?

_____

_____

JOURNAL ENTRY

Write a prayer in your own words concerning the truth you learned today:

_____

_____

_____

_____

_____

What is the main truth that you learned from today's devotion?

_____

_____

_____

_____

_____

you are righteous

Day 3
I Am Destined to Reign

But the fruit of the [Holy] Spirit [the work which His presence within accomplishes] is love, joy (gladness), peace, patience…, kindness, goodness…, faithfulness, gentleness (meekness, humility) [and] self-control. — Galatians 5:22-23 AMP

Over the past two days, you've learned that you are a righteous princess in the kingdom of God because of Jesus. The verses above describe the godly character that you have within you. They reveal that it's not you who brings this fruit out in your life by trying to be good; it is the power of the Holy Spirit that brings it out as you believe who you are in Jesus. That's why the devil tries so hard to get you to believe his lies. Here are some more of them you've probably heard:

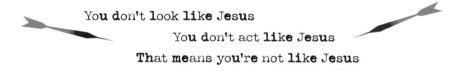

You don't look like Jesus

You don't act like Jesus

That means you're not like Jesus

Have you seen the movie *The Princess Diaries*? The story is about a girl, Mia, who really is a princess, but doesn't know it. Because she has a negative opinion of herself, she feels awkward, ugly, clumsy and unpopular. Even though she really is a princess on the inside, she doesn't look like or act like one on the outside, because she doesn't believe who she really is.

One day her grandmother, Queen Clarisse Renaldi, comes to visit Mia and tells her that she is the daughter of the king of the country of Genovia, and that she is a genuine princess. At first, Mia has a hard time believing the truth, because all she can see is the common girl in the mirror. The Queen begins to teach her how to act like a princess: how a princess would carry herself and dress. Mia tries really hard to please her grandmother, but she ends up failing because in her heart she still believes that she'll never measure up to her grandmother's expectations and will just let everyone down. You see, no matter how much her grandmother believes in her, Mia does not believe the truth about herself.

Then one day she finds a letter from her father. In her father's loving letter, he encourages Mia to believe that she really is a genuine princess, and that she has a destiny to fulfill, to rule and reign over Genovia. Her father's words touch her heart, and as a result, Mia starts to believe the truth. She begins to see herself as the beautiful, confident, and capable princess she really is, and she is changed from the inside out. Everyone is amazed at the transformation in her life and she does end up reigning as the crown princess of Genovia.

This story is no different than your own. Jesus made you a genuine princess in His kingdom, but you don't have to try hard to act like one. Just like Mia in the *Princess Diaries*, you must only believe what your Heavenly Father says about you. Like Mia's grandmother, Jesus has sent the Holy Spirit to tell you who you really are and to help you bear the fruit of a righteous princess. When you daily trust Jesus, the Holy Spirit is the power within you to bring out the fruit of love, joy, and peace in your life.

Philippians 2:13 says, *For God is working in you, giving you the desire and the power to do what pleases Him.*

Colossians 1:21-23 says ...*you...were once so far away from God... yet now [Jesus] has brought you back as his friends. He has done this through his death on the cross... As a result, he has brought you into the very presence of God and you are holy and blameless as you stand before him without a single fault. But you must continue to believe this truth and stand in it firmly.* NLT

THIS IS WHAT YOUR HEAVENLY FATHER SAYS TO YOU

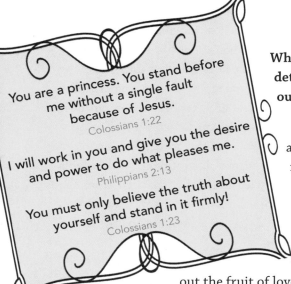

You are a princess. You stand before me without a single fault because of Jesus.
Colossians 1:22

I will work in you and give you the desire and power to do what pleases me.
Philippians 2:13

You must only believe the truth about yourself and stand in it firmly!
Colossians 1:23

What you believe about yourself determines the fruit that comes out in your life

I used to believe the devil's lies and just like Mia, I felt bad about myself and did not act like the righteous princess that Jesus had made me to be. As I started believing the truth that my Heavenly Father says about me, the Spirit of God began to bring out the fruit of love, joy and peace in my life.

The same is true for you. As you choose to believe what your Heavenly Father says about you, you'll reign as the princess in the kingdom of God that you were destined to be.

So believe what your Heavenly Father says about you. Speak the truth out loud:

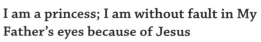

- **I am a princess; I am without fault in My Father's eyes because of Jesus**
- **God works in me and gives me the desire and power to do what pleases Him**
- **I believe the truth of who I am in Jesus**

PRAYER: *Heavenly Father, I know You love me because You made me a princess through Jesus. I now understand that it is the Holy Spirit Who brings the fruit of Godly character out in my life when I simply believe who I am in Jesus. Help me to believe what Jesus says about me. Thank You for working in me and giving me the desire and power to do what pleases You. Thank You for making it so easy for me, all I have to do is believe what You say! You really do love me!*

STUDY QUESTIONS

Now that you've discovered that you are a princess in God's kingdom, have any of these negative lies come to your mind:

LIES EXPOSED

You don't look like a princess	_____Yes	_____ No
You don't act like a princess	_____Yes	_____ No
That means you're not a princess	_____Yes	_____ No

Why do you think the devil does not want you to believe that you're a righteous princess?_____

_____

NOW LET'S STUDY THE TRUTH TOGETHER

Read **Colossians 1:21-23:** *²¹...you who were once so far away from God. You were his enemies, separated from him by your evil thoughts and actions. Yet now [Jesus] has brought you back as his friends. He has done this through his death on the cross in his own human body. ²² As a result, he has brought you into the very presence of God, and you are* <u>holy</u> *and* <u>blameless</u> *as you stand before him* <u>without a single fault</u>. *²³ But you must continue to believe this truth and stand in it firmly.* NLT

What do you look like to your Heavenly Father? Fill in the blanks from verse 22 above:

I am a righteous princess because of Jesus. He has brought me into the presence of God. I am _____ and _____ as I stand before Him without a single _____.

What does verse 23 tell you to do so that the fruit of a righteous princess will come out in your life?

_____

_____

Read **Philippians 2:13:** *For God is working in you, giving you the desire and the power to do what pleases him.*

As you look to Jesus for strength, what does He promise to do in you?

_____

_____

Now write **T** next to the statements that are true and **L** next to the statements that are lies:

_____ I don't look or act like a princess so I must not be one

_____ I am holy, blameless and without a single fault because of Jesus

_____ I need to try in my own strength to act like a princess

_____ The Holy Spirit gives me the desire and power to do
what pleases God

_____ I must only believe who I am in Jesus to experience
the fruit in my life

GOING DEEPER

TRUTH: **I am destined to reign through Jesus**

Read Romans 5:17 in your own Bible.
What does this verse say about those who receive God's grace and believe that they are righteous in Jesus?

_____

_____

Read Galatians 5:16-25.
Verses 19-21 say: *The wrong things the sinful self does are clear: being sexually unfaithful, not being pure, taking part in sexual sins, worshiping gods, doing witchcraft, hating, making trouble, being jealous, being angry, being selfish, making people angry with each other, causing divisions among people, feeling envy, being drunk, having wild and wasteful parties, and doing other things like these.* NCV

According to verses 19-21, if you believe the devil's lies and forget who you are in Jesus, what actions will your life produce?

_____

_____

How will these actions affect your life in a negative way?

_____

Now read verses 22-23: *But the fruit of the [Holy] Spirit [the work which His presence within accomplishes] is love, joy (gladness), peace, patience..., kindness, goodness..., faithfulness, gentleness (meekness, humility), [and] self-control.* AMP

What fruit does the Holy Spirit bring out in your life when you believe who you are in Jesus?

_____

_____

How will this fruit affect your life in a positive way?

_____

JOURNAL ENTRY

Write a prayer in your own words concerning the truth you have learned today.

_____

_____

_____

_____

What is the main truth that you learned from today's devotion?

_____

_____

_____

_____

_____

WEEK 2
THE
FEARLESS FACTOR
You're Loved
by Jesus

Connie Witter

Day 1
I Am Loved

Day 2
I Am Aware of the Enemy's Lies

Day 3
I Agree with Jesus

Day 1
I Am Loved

Long before he laid down earth's foundations, he had us in mind, had settled on us as the focus of his love, to be made whole and holy by his love. — *Ephesians 1:4* MSG

Long before the earth was even created, God had you on his mind. He wanted sons and daughters to love, so He created you and me for that purpose. He wanted to meet every need of our hearts and make our hearts whole by His love.

Since God put that need in all of our hearts to be completely accepted and loved, He's the only one who can truly fill it. When we find ourselves going outside of our relationship with Jesus to meet our need to be accepted, our hearts become broken.

When I was a teenager I looked to others for approval and love. I wanted people to love me and think good of me all the time. I looked to my parents and teachers, my friends, and even boyfriends to meet this need in my heart. But what this did, was create insecurity in me because other people's opinions of me changed all the time. If I behaved well, they were happy with me; if I didn't, they disapproved. Somehow I always ended up feeling sad and empty.

There is no one in this world who can make your heart truly whole except Jesus. **Ephesians 1:4** in the New Living Translation says, ***Even before he made the world, God loved us and chose us in Christ to be holy and without fault in his eyes.*** Your Heavenly Father is the only One who sees you as perfect and faultless 100% of the time because of Jesus. And He never changes His good opinion of you. That's why you can be completely secure in His love.

But the devil doesn't want you to feel complete in your relationship with Jesus so he speaks lies like these into your heart:

You need something else to feel complete
You lack in some way   You need man's approval to feel loved

Just like most of us have done, my oldest son Justin had an experience with a girlfriend, where he looked to her for love and approval. His heart was broken as he realized that no girl could fill the need in his heart to be completely loved. He wrote a beautiful song about his experience, which I would like to share with you in today's devotion:

Completes Me
By Justin Witter

Darkness consumed me for a time,
I kept things to myself all along.
You see what I've done to this heart of mine,
Your love for me, again, I must find.

A hole in my heart, I tried to fill;
I tried and tried, but it would not heal.
It took me sometime to realize
The only way to fill this void,

Is to run back to You,
'Cause You're all I need.
I'm running back to You
'Cause You're my everything.
I've been lost for a time, but now I see,
That only Your love completes me.

Many mistakes I've made so far,
Each of which I am not proud.
They haunted me again and again,
Until Your love I found within.

Your love filled my void,
I need search no more;
'Cause I know what I must do,
My joy is only found in You.

You died for me so I wouldn't need
To bear the burden of my many sins.
Your mercy and forgiveness grace my life
Revealing the beauty I hold within.

My life is now complete because
Of Your love, My Lord, My God.
You gave up Your Son for me,
Because of your grace I've been set free.

Lord Jesus, You're the only way,
To live a happy life,
I run back to You whenever I fall,
'Cause Your love completes me!

Colossians 2:9-10 says, *For in Christ lives all the fullness of God in a human body. So you also are complete through your union with Christ.* When you accepted Jesus as your Savior, you became complete in Him. You are completely accepted, approved, and loved by Him, and nothing will ever change His love for you (Romans 8:38-39)

Jesus is the Truth. Listen as He speaks His words of love to your heart…

You are complete in Me.
You lack nothing.
Colossians 2:9-10

You're perfect in my sight and My good opinion of you will never change.
Ephesians 1:4

Nothing will ever separate you from my love.
Romans 8:38-39

First **John 4:18** says, *Perfect love casts out all fear.*NKJV When you receive His words of love toward you, you'll live free from all fear. You can live securely in His love by turning your heart toward Him and agreeing with what He says about you. So, agree with the One who loves you and speak these truths out loud:

- ♥ **Jesus, I am complete in You; I lack nothing**
- ♥ **I'm perfect in Your sight and Your good opinion of me will never change**
- ♥ **Nothing can ever separate me from Your love**

PRAYER: *Lord, I know You love me because You made me perfect in Jesus. I now realize that only You can fill the need in my heart to be completely loved. Help me to believe what You say about me so I can live securely in You. I can live free from fear because of Your unchanging love for me. Thank You, for showing me that in You, I am complete.*

STUDY QUESTIONS

Has the devil ever tried to deceive you with these lies:

You need something else
to feel complete   _____Yes _____ No

You lack in some way   _____Yes _____ No

You need man's approval
to feel loved   _____Yes _____ No

LIES EXPOSED

NOW LET'S STUDY THE TRUTH TOGETHER

Read **Ephesians 1:4** in the Message Bible:

Long before he laid down earth's foundations, he had us in mind, had settled on us as the focus of his love, to be made whole and holy by his love.

Who is the focus of God's love?

_____

How will your heart be made whole?

_____

_____

_____

Now let's look at this same verse in the New Living Translation:

Even before he made the world, God loved us and chose us in Christ to be holy and without fault in his eyes.

How does your Heavenly Father see you because of Jesus?

_____

Will His opinion of you ever change?

_____

Read **Colossian 2:9-10** again:

For in Christ lives all the fullness of God in a human body. So you also are complete in your union with Christ.

According to this verse, do you lack in any way?

_____

Put your name in the blank below and say this truth to yourself:

For in Christ lives all the fullness of God in a human body.

So I, _____ am complete through my union with Christ.

Now write **T** next to the statements that are true and **L** next to the statements that are lies:

_____ I am complete in Jesus; I am perfect in His sight

_____ I lack in some way; I need something else to be happy

_____ People can fill the need in my heart to be completely loved

_____ I am completely accepted and loved by Jesus

_____ My bad behavior can cause God to change His opinion of me

_____ I'm secure in Jesus because nothing will ever separate me from His love

GOING DEEPER

TRUTH: I am completely loved by my Heavenly Father

Write down some of the names of people in your life that you have looked to for love and approval:

_____

_____

Did they always maintain their good opinion of you?

_____

How did it make you feel when they changed their opinion?

_____

Why does looking to another person for approval cause insecurity in your heart?

_____

_____

Read **1 John 4:16-19** in your own Bible.

Look at verse 18 again. What casts out all insecurity and fear from your heart?

_____

Read **Romans 8:38-39.**
Jesus always has a good opinion of you and His love never changes. How does knowing that help you experience security in His love?

_____

_____

JOURNAL ENTRY

Write a prayer or poem in your own words concerning the truth you learned today:

_____

_____

_____

_____

_____

What is the main truth that you learned from today's devotion?

_____

_____

_____

_____

_____

Day 2
I Am Aware of the Enemy's Lies

The thief comes only in order to steal and kill and destroy. I came that they may have and enjoy life, and have it in abundance (to the full, till it overflows). — *John 10:10* AMP

Just like what happens in almost every princess story, this verse reveals to us that there are two opposing forces that would like to see their plan fulfilled in your life. Jesus — your Prince — came to give you a wonderful, happy life by making your heart whole with His love. In contrast, the devil — your enemy — hates you because you're the daughter of the King of kings. He comes to steal, kill, and destroy your life by hurting your heart with his lies.

In **2 Corinthians 11:2-3,** the Apostle Paul said, *I am jealous for you with a godly jealousy. I promised you to one husband, to Christ, so that I might present you as a pure virgin to him. But I am afraid that just as Eve was deceived by the serpent's cunning, your minds may somehow be led astray from your sincere and pure devotion to Christ.* NIV

In this verse, the apostle Paul was saying that he has presented you to Jesus as His bride. Jesus loves you and He thinks you're perfect and wonderful. But Paul was concerned that just as the devil deceived Eve by telling her, *Something is wrong with you,* he would come and corrupt your mind with this same lie and take your heart away from your devotion to Jesus.

John 8:44, says, *"...the Devil .... was a murderer from the beginning. He has always hated the truth, because there is no truth in him. When he lies, it is consistent with his character, for he is a liar and the father of lies,"* and **Ephesians 6:16** says, *In every battle you will need faith as your shield to stop the fiery arrows aimed at you by Satan.* NLT

This scripture reveals that the fiery arrows the devil throws at you are lies. When you believe the lies of the enemy, your heart becomes broken, which is exactly the devil's plan for you. From the time we can understand, he begins throwing these lies at our hearts. Here are some of the ones you may have heard:

The symptoms of believing a lie are negative emotions

When you agree with the enemy's lies, they are like fiery darts which go into your heart and create brokenness. When you accept these lies as the truth, it creates a negative image of yourself, and produces negative emotions such as condemnation, worry, guilt, discouragement, depression, offense, insecurity, and fear. Whenever you have these negative feelings in your heart, you can know you are listening to a lie of the devil.

Unfortunately, the devil often uses other people to speak his lies to our hearts. As a young girl, I remember a group of boys making fun of me for the way I looked. Their negative words reinforced the lie I believed that I wasn't pretty enough and it made my heart very sad. Fortunately, as I stood there listening to them, my mom came to my rescue — just like Jesus does — with words of truth. I heard her say to those boys, "You just watch. Connie will grow up to be a beautiful swan." I remember looking up at her and receiving her loving words into my heart. Jesus used my mom to remind me of what He said about me. As I thought upon the truth, I was able to walk away from that situation encouraged instead of hurt.

The devil comes to break your heart with his lies, but Jesus came to heal your broken heart with the truth of His love (Isaiah 61:1-3). He came to set you free from every negative emotion.

Ephesians 6:16 says that you can stop all the fiery darts aimed at you by Satan by using the shield of faith. The shield of faith is simply agreeing with Jesus and believing what He says about you. So the next time you hear the devil's negative, lying thoughts in your mind that make your heart feel fearful or sad, put up your shield of faith by saying, "Talk to the hand devil, 'cuz the heart ain't listening!" Turn your thoughts to Jesus and ask Him to help you believe what He says.

PRAYER: *Heavenly Father, thank You for making me aware of the enemy's lies. I now know that when my heart feels sad or fearful, it's because the enemy is trying to get me to believe his lies. With Your help, though, I can resist the devil and believe You instead. I can live free from a negative self-image by agreeing with what You say about me. I know You love me because Jesus came to give me a happy heart and a blessed life.*

STUDY QUESTIONS

Look back at the heart in today's devotion. Has the devil ever tried to throw those same lies at your heart? Which ones stand out to you the most? _____

_____

NOW LET'S STUDY THE TRUTH TOGETHER

Read **John 10:10**: *The thief comes only in order to steal and kill and destroy. I came that they might have and enjoy life and have it in abundance (to the full, till it overflows).* AMP

What plan does the devil have for your life?

_____

What kind of life did Jesus come to give you?

_____

John 8:44, says, *"... the Devil .... was a murderer from the beginning. He has always hated the truth, because there is no truth in him. When he lies, it is consistent with his character; for he is a liar and the father of lies."*

What is the character of the devil? What is he called?

_____

Ephesians 6:16 says, *In every battle you will need faith as your shield to stop the fiery arrows aimed at you by Satan.* NLT

How can you stop the fiery lies that are aimed at your heart by Satan?

_____

What will you do the next time your heart feels sad or fearful?

_____

In **John 8:31, 32**: Jesus said, *"If you abide in My word..., you are truly My disciples. And you will know the Truth, and the Truth will set you free."* AMP
How can you live free from believing the devil's lies?

_____

Now write **T** next to the statements that are true and **L** next to the statements that are lies:

_____When I believe the devil's lie, I experience pain in my heart

_____When I believe Jesus, my heart is made whole with his love

_____ Believing lies won't hurt me

_____What the world says about me is true

_____The symptoms of believing a lie are negative emotions

_____When I resist the devil and turn to Jesus I'll live
        free from negative emotions

GOING DEEPER

TRUTH: Believing a lie produces negative emotions; believing the truth sets my heart free

Read **2 Corinthians 11:2-3** in your own Bible.
What was the Apostle Paul afraid of for you?

_____

The devil is called *"the father of lies."* How can you know when you're listening to the devil's lies? How do they make your heart feel?

_____

_____

Read **Isaiah 61:1-3.**
In verse 1 what does it say Jesus came to do about your heart?

_____

_____

Today, you learned that when you agree with Jesus, the devil's lies cannot penetrate your heart. However, sometimes we've agreed with the devil for so long, it's a little harder to resist his lies. Sometimes asking Jesus for "help," is the greatest prayer you can pray.

JOURNAL ENTRY

Write a short prayer in your own words asking Jesus for help to believe the truth:

_____

_____

_____

What is the main truth that you learned from today's devotion?

_____

_____

_____

Day 3
I Agree with Jesus

May Christ through your faith [actually] dwell ... in your hearts!
May you be rooted deep in love and founded securely on love. Now
to Him Who, by...the [action of His] power that is at work within
us, is able to [carry out His purpose and] do superabundantly, far
over and above all that we [dare] ask or think [infinitely beyond our
highest prayers, desires, thoughts, hopes, or dreams].
— *Ephesians 3:17, 20* AMP

Jesus has a wonderful plan for your life. These verses reveal that when you believe Jesus, His power, which is called *grace* is at work in your heart and he is able to bring to pass his plan for you. In our last study we took a look at some of the lies that the devil throws at your heart. When you agree with his lies about you, your heart becomes sad and broken. Jesus, however, always tells you the truth, and He says the exact opposite of what the devil says. His words bring freedom, peace, joy, and happiness to your heart (John 15:11). Jesus came to heal your heart with the Good News of His love and acceptance (Isaiah 61:1-3).

Because of your faith in Him, this is what Jesus says to you:

"You are a success" 2 Corinthians 2:14

"You are capable. You can do all things through Me" Philippians 4:13

"You're just like Me." 1 John 4:17

"You are valuable because I paid a great price for you" 1 Peter 1:18-19

"You are perfect in My sight" Ephesians 1:4

"I will never be angry with you" Isaiah 54:9-10

"You are qualified for all of My promises" Colossians 1:12

"You are forgiven. I don't remember any of your sins" Hebrews 8:12

"I love you completely. Nothing will ever change My love for you" Romans 8:38-39

"You are complete in Me. There is nothing lacking in you" Colossians 2:10

"I accept and approve of you" Ephesians 1:6

"You are wonderful! My thoughts about you are precious" Psalm 139:13-14, 17-18

"You are beautiful, My beloved, there is no flaw in you" Song of Songs 4:7

"You are favored" Psalm 5:12

"You are wise and smart" 1 Corinthians 2:16

security

wholeness

fearless/courage

strength

peace

love

complete

confidence

happiness

faith

joy

The fruit of believing Jesus is a happy heart

One day my youngest daughter, Victoria, was playing with a group of girls when one of them called her a "chicken head." Tearfully, she ran to me and asked me to "go tell that girl she wasn't a chicken head!" Instead, I looked her straight in the eye and said, "Victoria, is what that little girl said about you true? Are you really a chicken head? What does Jesus say about you?"

She looked up at me and responded, "Jesus says I'm beautiful, wonderful, and precious."

"That's right," I replied, "and we have a decision to make. Who are we going to believe? Are we going to believe that girl or are we going to believe Jesus?" "I'm going to believe Jesus!" she declared.

"That's wonderful," I responded with a big smile, "because when we believe Jesus it doesn't matter what that girl or anybody else says. We can be around people who may not even like us, and because we agree with Jesus, their opinion doesn't have any effect on us at all." Happily, she ran off to play and enjoyed the rest of the day.

I had a similar situation happen in my own life. One time I had a friend who got really upset with me and told me how horrible I was. She told me my heart was wrong and that it might be better if I just left and never came back. Her words cut into my heart like a knife. I couldn't believe she was saying such judgmental and critical things about me. I thought she was my friend. As tears rolled down my face, I told her I was sorry for anything I may have said that hurt her, but it didn't change the way she felt about me. I left our conversation feeling badly. The enemy had used her to throw his fiery darts at my heart to make me feel like I was a bad person and that something was wrong with me.

I took my heart to Jesus and talked to Him about how hurt I was. I asked Him to help me believe what He said about me. He reminded me that He thought I was wonderful and that I had a good heart, just like His. As I thought about what Jesus said about me and His precious thoughts toward me, His love began to heal my broken heart. The hurt I felt began to melt away, and I began to feel compassion rise up in my heart for my friend.

It's comforting to know that no matter what anyone else thinks of you, your Heavenly Father's good opinion of you never changes, because of Jesus. And what He says is always the truth. As you learn to run to Him for help whenever you feel disapproved of, or rejected, and you agree with what He says about you, you'll live free from the devil's lies and their effect on you. That is true freedom; to be able to walk around in this world and not be affected by anyone's opinion of you because you know who you are. You have the favor of God; you are approved by the King of kings; you are a princess in the kingdom of God. You are special, valuable, wonderful, and loved unconditionally. When you look to Jesus and agree with what He says about you, you'll experience His good plan for your life. Your heart will be filled with joy and peace. You'll live fearless, confident, and secure in His love.

PRAYER: *Jesus, I know that You love me. Your love fills all the needs of my heart. Help me to agree with what You say about me so that I can experience Your wonderful plan for my life. I am beautiful, valuable, wonderful, and favored because of You, Jesus. Thank You for loving me so much!*

STUDY QUESTIONS

Read **Ephesians 3:17 and 20:** *"[17]May Christ through your faith [actually] dwell… in your hearts! May you be rooted deep in love and founded securely on love. [20] Now to Him Who, by…the [action of His] power that is at work within us, is able to [carry out His purpose and] do superabundantly, far over and above all that we [dare] ask or think [infinitely beyond our highest prayers, desires, thoughts, hopes, or dreams].* AMP

NOW LET'S STUDY THE TRUTH TOGETHER

When you agree with Jesus, His power which is called *grace*, is at work in your heart. What does verse 20 say He is able to do in your life when you agree with Him?

_____

Look back at the heart in today's devotion. Listen, again as Jesus speaks His words of truth to your heart. Agree with Jesus and fill in the blanks below with the truth that encouraged you the most:
Because of Jesus,

    I am _____

    I am _____

    I am _____

    I am _____

    I am _____

    I am _____

I am _____

Now write **T** next to the statements that are true and **L** next to the statements that are lies:

_____ Jesus helps me agree with what He says about me

_____ I am a failure

_____ I am a success because of Jesus

_____ I am ugly

_____ I am beautiful in Jesus

_____ I am rejected; I don't belong

_____ I am accepted and completely loved by Jesus

GOING DEEPER

TRUTH: When I agree with Jesus, I will experience God's plan for my life

Have you had an experience where someone said something negative about you?

_____

_____

How did that make your heart feel? What lie were you tempted to believe?

_____

_____

Even though you may have believed that lie in the past, you can resist it now. What does Jesus say about you?

_____

_____

Say that truth out loud to yourself. How does your heart feel now that you have accepted the truth of what Jesus says about you?

_____

_____

Read **John 15:11** in your own Bible.

Why does Jesus speak His words of love to your heart?

_____

_____

How will believing the lies of the devil affect your life?

_____

_____

How will believing the truth of what Jesus says about you affect your life?

_____

_____

JOURNAL ENTRY

Write a short prayer in your own words concerning the truth you learned today:

_____

_____

_____

_____

_____

What is the main truth that you learned from today's devotion?

_____

_____

_____

_____

wonderful

forgiven

wise

loved

righteous

beautiful

perfect

complete

qualified

favored

WEEK 3

ARE YOU SMARTER THAN A FIFTH GRADER?

You Are Wise Because of Jesus

Kelly Ray

Day 1
I Am Wise

Day 2
I Am Led by God's Spirit

Day 3
I Am Confident

Day 1
I Am Wise

But to those who are called...Christ [is] the Power...and the Wisdom of God. — *I Corinthians 1:24* AMP

Life is full of choices. Every day we're faced with opportunities to choose which activities we're going to participate in and the people we're going to hang around with. God has given each of us the power to choose between life and death.

In **Deuteronomy 30:19** Jesus actually told us we have this power, *"Today I have given you the choice between life and death, between blessings and curses. I call on heaven and earth to witness the choice you make. Oh, that you would choose life, that you and your descendents might live"*. In **John 14:6** Jesus said, *"I am the way, the truth and the life."* So you see, when you choose Jesus, you are choosing life. The Bible tells us in **1 Corinthians 1:24** above that Jesus is the power and wisdom of God. Since Jesus lives in you, you are wise and you have His power to make good choices and enjoy a blessed and happy life.

Now, the enemy of your soul would like to do you harm and he knows that if you choose to do certain activities even though they seem like fun at first, they will ultimately bring you heartache and pain. He uses the same lies on everyone to tempt us to make bad choices. Have you ever heard these negative, lying thoughts in your mind:

I need to do what others are doing
to be accepted and have fun

My choices aren't important;
they don't affect anyone but me

My way is better than God's way

As a teenager, I did not realize that I was believing the devil's lies. As captain of my cheerleading squad, I had lots of opportunities to go places and do things with my friends. The devil lied to me and told me that to be popular, I needed to get involved in certain activities. If alcohol, drugs or smoking were offered I would give in and participate. Because I did not know that I was accepted and approved of by Jesus, I allowed myself to get involved in these activities, even though they were harmful. I was trying to please others and be accepted by those around me by doing what they wanted me to do. The devil lied to me by telling me that my choices weren't harmful and didn't affect anyone but me.

After a while, I began to think that what I was doing was okay. I frequently hung around with the crowds that smoked and drank because I felt accepted by them. On one particularly busy school day, a circle of people were doing drugs, and I was right there in the middle. I had been able to fool a lot of people for a long time, but on that eventful day the coach of the football team must have seen what I was doing. Disappointed, he walked right up and with his finger pointed at me, got right in my face and said, "You're supposed to be a leader among your friends. How can you lead so many people astray by your actions?" That was definitely an "Uh, oh!" moment for me; I was busted. In a flash, I realized the truth that what I do does matter – and that my choices and actions DO have an effect on others around me. As a result, that day I made the choice that I would no longer allow drugs to be part of my life.

Today I'm still tempted to please others but I no longer go along with what they think. I turn my thoughts to Jesus and ask for wisdom and I listen to what He says...

For years the hardest thing to change was my reputation. I didn't want to be labeled a druggy, alcoholic, or smoker, even though that's what my actions led others to believe about me. I needed someone to redeem my reputation. The Good News is that

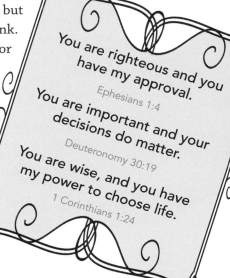

You are righteous and you have my approval.
Ephesians 1:4

You are important and your decisions do matter.
Deuteronomy 30:19

You are wise, and you have my power to choose life.
1 Corinthians 1:24

two thousand years ago, Jesus did that exact thing for me by taking on Himself every foolish decision I would ever make and giving me his right decisions — His wisdom and his righteousness in their place. He erased all my mistakes. I now have the reputation of being wise because I look to Jesus and He gives me the power to choose life!

Today you can decide to believe the lies of the enemy and choose death or you can choose to believe Jesus. He says, *"I set before you life and death. Now choose life."* When you believe Jesus, you are choosing life. He is the wisdom of God. So say the truth out loud:

- ♥ **I am righteous and approved by my Heavenly Father**

- ♥ **My life is important, and my decisions do matter**

- ♥ **I am wise because Jesus lives in me, and He gives me the power to make good choices**

PRAYER: *Thank you, Lord, for giving me the power to choose life! When I believe what You say about me, Your plan comes to pass in my life. When I'm tempted to make a bad decision, I can turn to You and receive Your wisdom. You'll give me the power to believe what You say and to do what's right. I am righteous and I don't have to do harmful things to be accepted because You accept me! You live in me, and I am wise because of You. I choose life because I choose You, Jesus!*

STUDY QUESTIONS

Have you ever had these negative lying thoughts before:

I need to do what others are doing to be accepted and have fun   _____Yes _____ No

My choices aren't important; they don't affect anyone but me   _____Yes _____ No

My way is better than God's way   _____Yes _____ No

LIES EXPOSED

NOW LET'S STUDY THE TRUTH TOGETHER

Read **Deuteronomy 30:19**: *"Today I have given you the choice between life and death, between blessings and curses. Now I call on heaven and earth to witness the choice you make. Oh, that you would choose life, so that you and your descendants might live!"*

In the above scripture, what two choices does God give you? What does Jesus encourage you to choose? Why?

_____

_____

Read **John 14:6**: *Jesus told him, "I am the way, the truth and the life."*
What does Jesus say about Himself in this Scripture?

_____

Read **1 Corinthians 1:24**: *But to those who are called . . . Christ [is] the Power . . . and the Wisdom of God.* AMP
In this Scripture, what two things is Jesus called?

_____   _____

Since Jesus lives in you, what two things do you have inside you to help you make good choices?

_____   _____

Write **T** next to the statements that are true, and **L** next to the statements that are lies:

_____ My way is better than God's way

_____ I need to do what others are doing to be accepted and have fun

_____ My decisions are not important

_____ I am an important leader in God's kingdom and my choices do affect others

_____ Jesus gives me the wisdom and power to make good choices and enjoy a blessed and happy life

_____ I am wise because Jesus lives in me

GOING DEEPER

TRUTH: I am wise because Jesus lives in me

The devil would like you to make bad choices by believing negative things about yourself. Have you ever made a bad choice and did something you knew was wrong? Explain:

_____

_____

Before you made that choice, what negative lie did you believe?

_____

_____

What negative feelings did you have after you made that choice?

_____

_____

As a result of what you chose, did it affect your reputation with others in any way?

_____

_____

Read **Ephesians 1:4.**
What did Jesus do on the cross about your reputation? According to this verse, how does your Heavenly Father see you because of Jesus?

_____

_____

Read **Hebrews 8:12.**
What does Jesus do with all your mistakes? What should you do with your mistakes?

_____

_____

Read **Hebrews 4:14-16.**

According to verse 16, where can you go when you're tempted to make a bad choice? What will Jesus give you to help you make a wise choice?

_____

_____

JOURNAL ENTRY

In your own words, write a prayer to Jesus concerning what you learned today:

_____

_____

_____

_____

_____

What is the main truth that you learned from today's devotion?

_____

_____

_____

_____

_____

Day 2

I Am Led by God's Spirit

"No eye has seen, no ear has heard, and no mind has imagined what God has prepared for those who love him." But it was to us that God revealed these things by his Spirit. For his Spirit searches out everything and shows us God's deep secrets.

— *I Corinthians 2:9-10*

In our last devotion, we learned that Jesus has given us His wisdom and power to make good choices. In life we will also have to decide such things as who to date and what we will do for a career. We often think we know what's best, but we cannot see into the future and relying on our education, experience and desires does not guarantee success. Wouldn't it be great if there was someone you could go to who knows everything from start to finish and all the in-between? Well, the Good News is that there is, but He's not someone with a crystal ball who claims to be psychic. The scripture says our Heavenly Father has made His secrets available to us through His Son Jesus Christ. In **Colossians 2:3** it says *In Him all the treasures of wisdom and knowledge are hidden.* HCSB The nice thing is, we don't have to go anywhere or pay anything; we can find out what to do by simply turning our thoughts to Jesus and asking for His help. If you ask Him for wisdom, He will give it to you (James 1:5).

But your enemy, the devil, wants you to live in confusion so he attempts to get you to believe these lies:

I can't **hear God's voice**

I am so confused, I don't know **what to do**

I can't **figure this** out; it's too **hard**

I remember walking in the mall one day with a friend, when we came upon a lady claiming the ability to predict our futures by reading tarot cards. We were both curious, so we paid her some money and let her tell us our future. Afterwards we were disappointed as we realized that the "secrets" she told us were so vague they could be applied to just about anyone. We had wasted all that time and money on useless information, when we could have gone to Jesus for something so much deeper that wouldn't have cost us a dime. We fell for this scam because we bought into the lie that we couldn't hear from Jesus.

All of us, at one time or another, have gotten so busy with activities, that we have missed how simple and easy it is to be led by God's Spirit. **Romans 8:14** says, *All who are led by the Spirit of God are children of God.* Here is the truth of what Jesus says to you . . .

I remember a time when I was dating a guy for a couple of months, and things were going quite well; we had similar interests and enjoyed each other's company. One day as I was praying about the next step in our relationship, I asked Jesus if he was the one for me, and whether I should continue dating him. **Proverbs 3:5-6** describes what happens when you look to Jesus for guidance for your life. *Trust in the LORD with all your heart; do not depend on your own understanding. Seek his will in all you do, and he will show you which path to take.* As I waited, I quietly heard these words in my heart, *You have to give him up,* and *drugs.* Well, this was not the response I wanted to hear. I had not seen any sign of drugs and he told me he was not using them. I realized what I had to do, but because I cared for him, I asked Jesus to help me and protect both our hearts so neither of us would be hurt.

You hear my voice and the voice of a stranger you will not follow.
John 10:4-5

I will lead you in the way you should go.
Proverbs 3:5-6

You're my daughter and I will lead you by my Spirit.
Romans 8:14

Later on over lunch, I asked him if everything was okay, as he seemed distracted and distant. I thought maybe he was interested in dating other people. In answer to my question, he revealed to me that things had changed with him; that he was not interested in *someone* else, but *something* else; he had relapsed into drug addiction. His advice was for me to "move on and not look back." Even though what he said made me sad, Jesus had already prepared my heart. I knew the best thing would be for me to give him up to Jesus and let Him deal with my friend's issues. I continued to pray for him, but eventually lost contact.

When you look to Jesus for guidance, He'll show you what to do and help you do it. He may even tell you something you don't want to hear because He loves you and knows what's best for you. He doesn't want to see you hurt. We can't always see into the future, but Jesus can, and He'll prepare your heart to deal with anything that may come up. So take every part of your life to Jesus. Ask Him to tell you what He thinks about the matter; then agree with Him, because He loves you. Say these truths out loud:

> ♥ **I hear Your voice, Jesus, and I follow You**
> ♥ **You will show me the right way to go**
> ♥ **I am led by Your Spirit**

PRAYER: *Thank You, Jesus, for showing me that I do hear Your voice and that You do help me to make the right decisions. I don't have to try and figure things out on my own. I can look to You and You will lead me by your Spirit. I know I can trust You because You love me so much.*

STUDY QUESTIONS

Have you ever been tempted to believe these lies?

I can't **hear** God's **voice**   _____Yes _____ No

I am so con**fused**; I don't
know what to do   _____Yes _____ No

I'll **never be able** to **figure**
this out; it's **too hard**   _____Yes _____ No

LIES EXPOSED

Read **Romans 1:25**: *They traded the truth about God for a lie. So they worshiped and served the things God created instead of the Creator himself.*

According to this scripture, when we believe the enemy we are exchanging the truth for what?

_____

NOW LET'S STUDY THE TRUTH TOGETHER

Read **1 Corinthians 2:9-10**: *"No eye has seen, no ear has heard, and no mind has imagined what God has prepared for those who love him." 10 But it was to us that God revealed these things by his Spirit. For his Spirit searches out everything and shows us God's deep secrets.*

What does the Spirit search out?

_____

What does the Spirit show us?

_____

Do we need to go to other people to find out what our future holds? Why or why not?

_____

_____

Read **Romans 8:14**: *All who are led by the Spirit of God are children of God.*

What two things does this verse say about you?

_____

_____

Write **T** next to the statements that are true and **L** next to the statements that are lies:

_____ I have to figure things out on my own

_____ When I ask Jesus, He will show me what to do in every situation

_____ I can't hear God's voice

_____ I hear God's voice and the voice of a stranger I will not follow

_____ I am led by His Spirit because of Jesus

GOING DEEPER

TRUTH: I am led by God's Spirit

Have you recently had decisions you needed to make for your life? Possibly concerning a friend, a boyfriend, school, classes, college, or your future? Explain:

_____

_____

_____

Have you found yourself worried that you might make a wrong choice? What negative thoughts have you had that have caused you to be fearful?

_____

_____

Read **Proverbs 3:5-6.**
What promise does God give you in these verses?

_____

_____

Read **John 10:4-5**
You are God's sheep, what does this verse say about you?

_____

_____

JOURNAL ENTRY

In your own words, write a prayer concerning what you learned today:

What is the main truth that you learned from today's devotion?

you are led by God's Spirit

Day 3
I Am Confident

I have told you these things, so that in Me you may have [perfect] peace and confidence. — *John 16:33* AMP

So far, you've learned that because Jesus lives in you, you have His wisdom and power to make good choices for your life. As a daughter of God, you hear His voice and are led by His Spirit. Jesus speaks the truth to you so that in Him you can have perfect peace and confidence. He wants you to be a confident person. The definition of *confidence* is "freedom from doubt; a feeling of trust in someone or something; a state of confident hopefulness that things will be favorable."[2] We need confidence the most when an outcome is uncertain.

On the flip side, we lack confidence because we are afraid that we will fail. **2 Timothy 1:7** tells us that *God has not given us a spirit of fear and timidity, but of power, love, and self-discipline.* NLT Fear does not come from our Heavenly Father. When we're afraid, it's because we are believing the lies of the enemy. Have you ever had these negative thoughts enter your mind:

I'm not smart enough

I can't do it; what if I fail?

I have to trust in myself

There are two kinds of confidence: self-confidence and confidence in God. *Self-confidence* is a "belief in yourself and your own power and ability outside of God".[3] It's trusting in yourself to succeed. Self-confidence is a term used to describe how secure a person is in their own decisions and actions. Trusting in your "self" is the world's way of thinking and will leave you disappointed and discouraged.

When I was a young girl, I thought if I were smart enough, pretty enough and good enough, that would be enough for me to be loved and accepted. So I worked really hard at everything I did, and each time I achieved a goal or performed well I thought that would make me more loveable. I believed that I would eventually reach perfection and everything would work out great for me. I was constantly trying to prove to others and myself that I could accomplish anything if I put my mind to it.

Occasionally, I would fail, but I learned to maintain my self-confidence by shifting the blame for the failure on someone else. Covering up and pretending helped me continue my game of "self-confidence." It all seemed to be working out pretty well until an important relationship I had with someone I loved failed. In an attempt to maintain my self-confidence, I desperately tried to fix the relationship, but it still fell apart. I became depressed and discouraged with thoughts of suicide, and I realized that being confident in myself was not a guarantee of success! Even though I had tried to do everything right, it still had not worked out. How could anyone — especially God — love such a failure? I was devastated.

Although this situation caused me much pain, it actually became a turning point in my life. As I cried out to Jesus for help, he began to work on my behalf. He showed me that I had been relying on myself instead of Him. I decided to place my confidence in Him and not my "self" any longer. As I began to choose His life, listen to His voice, and trust Him to work out His plan for my life, things began to change for the better.

True confidence comes only from knowing the truth God speaks to our hearts and relying on His ability on the inside of us. As we look to Him and agree with what He says, He gives us the ability to succeed. Listen to the truth that Jesus speaks to your heart . . .

Proverbs 16:3 says, *Roll your works upon the Lord [commit and trust them wholly to Him; He will cause your thoughts to become agreeable to His will, and] so shall your plans be*

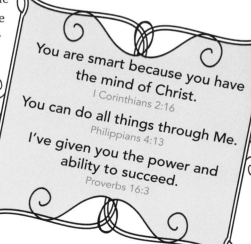

You are smart because you have the mind of Christ.
I Corinthians 2:16

You can do all things through Me.
Philippians 4:13

I've given you the power and ability to succeed.
Proverbs 16:3

established and succeed. AMP As you begin to agree with Jesus, his power of grace will help you succeed. He doesn't expect you to do it on your own. He will guide you, lead you and never abandon you. This is where true confidence comes from. Your confidence is in Him and His promise to you. This is the simple and easy way to live.

So agree with the One who loves you, and say the truth out loud:

♥ **I am smart; I have the mind of Christ**

♥ **I can do all things through Jesus**

♥ **I am confident that Jesus will help me succeed**

PRAYER: *Thank You, Jesus for loving me so much. I believe You and trust You to help me succeed. I know that I can be confident in You and Your ability in me. You have not given me a spirit of fear, but a spirit of power, love and a sound mind. I can be confident because I know You love me.*

STUDY QUESTIONS

Have you ever believed these lies:

LIES EXPOSED

I'm not smart enough	_____ Yes	_____ No
I can't do it. What if I fail?	_____ Yes	_____ No
I have to trust in myself to succeed	_____ Yes	_____ No

"Talk to the hand devil, 'cuz the heart ain't listening!"

"I believe what Jesus says about me!"

NOW LET'S STUDY THE TRUTH TOGETHER

Read **1 Corinthians 2:16:** *But we have the mind of Christ.* KJV
What does this verse say about you? Why do you have the wisdom you need to succeed?

_____

_____

Read **Proverbs 16:3:** *Roll your works upon the Lord [commit and trust them wholly to Him; He will cause your thoughts to become agreeable to His will, and] so shall your plans be established and succeed.* AMP

What does this verse say that Jesus will do in your life when you trust Him?

_____

_____

Read **John 16:33:** *I have told you these things, so that in Me you may have [perfect] peace and confidence.* AMP

Why does Jesus speak the truth to your heart?

_____

_____

Write **T** next to the statements that are true and **L** next to the statements that are lies:

_____ I can do all things through Christ who strengthens me
_____ I have the mind of Christ
_____ I have to trust in my own ability to succeed
_____ I'm not smart enough; I can't do it
_____ Jesus will help me succeed
_____ I am confident in who I am in Jesus.

GOING DEEPER

TRUTH: I am confident because of Jesus

Read **Philippians 4:13.**

What does this verse say about you?

_____

_____

_____

Read **Romans 8:38-39.**

What can you be completely confident of?

_____

_____

_____

Write down some of the truths Jesus has spoken to you through the devotions you've done so far that give you peace and confidence:

_____

_____

_____

_____

_____

_____

_____

_____

_____

_____

JOURNAL ENTRY

Write a short prayer talking to Jesus about what you learned about placing your confidence in Him:

What is the main truth that you learned from today's devotion?

Jesus makes me confident

WEEK 4
AMERICA'S NEXT TOP MODEL
You're Beautiful Because of Jesus
Kelly Ray

Day 1
I Am Beautiful

Day 2
I Am Perfect

Day 3
I Am Beautiful Within

Day 1
I Am Beautiful

How beautiful you are, my beloved, how beautiful!
—*Song of Songs 4:1* NLT

God put the desire to be beautiful in every girl's heart, but from when we were young we've learned to measure our beauty by the picture-perfect girls we see in magazines and TV programs. Have you ever watched the series, *America's Next Top Model?* Many girls are drawn to this show because deep within their hearts, they want to feel beautiful, too. On the program, we watch as young women compete to become the next top model and have their picture on the cover of the top fashion magazines. As they walk across the runway in their beautiful designer clothing, we find ourselves secretly thinking *I wish I was as beautiful as those models are! If I were that perfect, I'd feel good about the way I looked.* The trap is that as long as we compare ourselves with others, we'll always feel like we don't quite measure up.

In Ezekiel 16:13-14 Jesus says that your beauty is made perfect by His *glory[4]*, which is His character in you and His opinion of you. That is what makes you beautiful, not makeup and hairstyles. As you continue to listen and agree with what Jesus says about you, you'll gain a confidence that the world can't take away, because His opinion is the only one that really matters.

In **Song of Songs 4:1** Jesus says ***"You are beautiful, my darling, beautiful beyond words."*** Jesus is saying that He loves you and He thinks that you are beautiful! The word *beautiful* means "very pleasing to see, lovely; delighting the senses."[5] Because of Jesus, when the Father looks at you, He sees those same excellent qualities in you. In His eyes you are delightful, lovely and pleasing; you are truly beautiful in His sight.

As we grow from young ladies to women, fast-paced changes happen in our minds and bodies. We go through growth spurts, complexion and weight changes as part of our development. These changes can cause us to have negative thoughts about ourselves. Even worse, at a time when we could really use some encouragement, people often say mean things that can cause us to think that there is something wrong with us. We've all had these hurtful experiences.

Once again, you must be aware that you have an enemy who wants you to believe his lies. Have you ever heard these hurtful, negative words before?

You're not pretty

You're too fat

Something is wrong with you

When I was a young girl, the devil threw these same fiery darts at my heart and unfortunately I believed them way longer than I should have. As with most growing teenagers, my body began to change. I became taller, rounder and gained some weight during this period of time. I became obsessed with my weight gain, and thinking I needed to lose weight, would starve myself for long periods of time. When I would eat, I'd only eat small portions to keep from gaining weight. You see, I had bought into the enemy's lie that there was something wrong with me. For many years, I struggled with low self-worth and an eating disorder because I believed I was fat.

Over time, I realized that I had believed a lie. I turned to Jesus and asked Him to forgive me for believing my own opinion over what He thought about me. I asked Him to help me believe the truth. When I did, He showed me that my beauty was not dependent on my size or my weight, but on what He said. Here is what He says to me from **Song of Songs 4:7:** *My darling, everything about you is beautiful, and there is nothing at all wrong with you.* NCV I began to listen to His comforting words and not the opinions of others. Jesus is the Truth, and this is what he says about me and you . . .

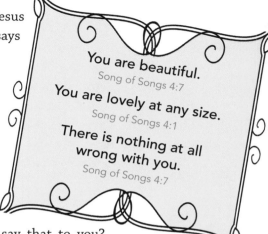

You are beautiful.
Song of Songs 4:7

You are lovely at any size.
Song of Songs 4:1

There is nothing at all wrong with you.
Song of Songs 4:7

Don't you love hearing Jesus say that to you? Don't His words bring peace and confidence to your heart? When I began to agree with the truth of what Jesus said about me, I was changed by His wonderful gift of love and grace. Jesus wants you to live free from the hurt and pain of a negative self-image. He wants you to believe what He thinks about you. The truth is, Jesus is your friend, and He always speaks the truth. You can go to Him anytime you're tempted to feel negative about the way you look. He is always there to remind you of the truth. No matter what anyone says, you delight and please Him, and He thinks you're beautiful! Whether you are having a bad hair day or wearing the latest fashion accessories; whether you're a size 2, 12 or 22, in Jesus' eyes you are beautiful and lovely. **Psalm 90:17** says ***The beauty and delightfulness and favor of the Lord our God [is] upon us.*** AMP Continue to turn to Him, and as you receive His love, you'll begin to love yourself and see the beauty in you, too.

So, let's agree with the One Who thinks we're beautiful! Speak these truths out loud:

♥ **I am beautiful**

♥ **I am lovely**

♥ **Jesus loves me and there is nothing at all wrong with me**

PRAYER: *Heavenly Father, thank You so much for showing me the truth about how You see me. I don't have to believe the lie that there's something wrong with me or that I have to look a certain way or be a certain size to be beautiful. I am beautiful because that's what You say about me, and You always speak the truth. When I'm tempted to believe Satan's lies, help me to turn to You to receive the power to believe only what You say about me: That in Your eyes, I am beautiful and lovely! Thank You, Lord, that You love me that much!*

STUDY QUESTIONS

Have you ever heard the devil speak these lies to your heart?

LIES EXPOSED

You're not **pretty enough**   _____ Yes _____ No

There's something **wrong with** you   _____ Yes _____ No

You're too fat   _____ Yes _____ No

How do these lies make you feel about yourself?

_____

_____

_____

NOW LET'S STUDY THE TRUTH TOGETHER

Read **Ezekiel 16:13b-14:** *You were very beautiful and became a queen. Then you became famous among the nations, because you were so beautiful. Your beauty was perfect, because of the glory I gave you, says the Lord God.* NCV

Write your name in the spaces below and say these words to yourself:

_____ **is very beautiful.**

_____ **is a queen**

The glory Jesus has given _____ **has made her beauty perfect.**

The word glory[4] means "the honor resulting from [God's] good opinion." Jesus has given you His glory and that makes you beautiful. The Hebrew meaning of the word *beautiful* is "to be bright," or to "shine, and to send out beams"[5] like a light that shines forth from a star. When we believe we are beautiful, we shine like a star and it has nothing to do with our size, our makeup, or the color of our hair. When we agree with Jesus' opinion of us, our brightness shines, and the peace, joy and confidence in our hearts affects those around us in a positive way.

Read **Song of Songs 4:7:** *My darling, everything about you is beautiful, and there is nothing at all wrong with you.* NCV
What does Jesus say about you in this verse? Fill in the blank below:

Everything about me is:_____

What does this Scripture say is wrong with you? _____

Write **T** next to the statements that are true and **L** next to the ones that are lies:

_____ Jesus thinks I'm lovely
_____ There is something wrong with me
_____ I am beautiful
_____ I'm too fat
_____ I'm not pretty enough
_____ There is nothing at all wrong with me

Say the statements marked **T** out loud.

GOING DEEPER

TRUTH: Jesus thinks I'm beautiful

Was there a time in your life when you felt you weren't beautiful? What lies did you believe that made you draw that conclusion?

_____

_____

What negative emotions did you experience as a result of believing those lies?

_____

_____

Jesus does not want us to experience negative emotions. Sometimes we look to others to tell us just how beautiful we are, which can be disappointing if they don't tell us what we want to hear. The important thing is to think about Jesus' opinion of us.

Read Song of Songs 4:7 in your Bible.

What does Jesus say about you in this verse?

_____

JOURNAL ENTRY

Write a short prayer asking Jesus to help you believe what He says about you:

_____

_____

_____

_____

_____

What is the main truth that you learned from today's devotion?

_____

_____

_____

_____

Day 2
I Am Perfect

"You are so beautiful, my beloved, so perfect in every part."
—*Song of Songs 4:7* NLT

We all have the desire to be perfect; to look and be our best at all times. But Jesus is the only one who can do that for us. In the above scripture, Jesus tells us that every part of you is perfect and that He thinks you're beautiful and loves you just the way you are. We often attempt to be perfect by trying to do it ourselves. If we're not perfect, we don't think we're beautiful. We measure ourselves by the world's standards of outward beauty. The models in the magazines and on shows like *America's Next Top Model* seem perfect. We think if we just looked like them we'd be beautiful. When we think this way, we are believing the devil's lies.

Have you ever had these negative thoughts go through your mind?

You're not **perfect enough**

No one thinks you're beautiful

You'd be beautiful if you looked like she does

As girls we love to go to the spa and get our hair fixed, our nails painted, and our faces all made-up. Pampering makes us feel uplifted, special, and better about ourselves for a time. Unfortunately, we all know that beauty treatments don't last. Looking in the mirror later on we notice that our make-up has faded and our hair doesn't look quite as nice. This can cause us to feel bad about ourselves, if we measure our beauty only from our outward appearance.

For a treat, I took my daughter's Bible study group for a day of pampering at the salon. They had a blast, and later celebrated with a party. Singing for each other and dancing, they pretended to be famous stars. But as with all wonderful events, the party was soon over and it was time to go home. As we got into the van, I noticed that their make-up was smeared; their nails had chipped and their hair had fallen. Even though their beauty treatments were fading, I saw a beauty in them that was much more lasting: the beginning stages of beautiful women of God. I could see in them the beauty that Jesus sees. The Bible tells us that men look at the outward appearance of a person, but Jesus looks at the heart. He thinks you're absolutely beautiful and from His point of view, your beauty never fades. In his eyes you are perfect through and through.

This is what Jesus says about you...

In **Matthew 5:48** Jesus says, *"But you are to be perfect, even as your Father in heaven is perfect."* You're probably thinking how could I ever be as perfect as God?

Jesus is our supermodel; He is the model of perfection. When you asked Jesus into your heart, He came to live in you. From that moment, you became just like Jesus, perfect in the Father's eyes. Simply believing in Jesus makes you beautiful and perfect. As you look to Him to meet your need to feel beautiful, you will reflect His image more and more. Every part of you was made from the most priceless treasure, Jesus. Therefore, you can be confident in your perfection. Let Jesus fulfill your desire for beauty and perfection and you will not be disappointed.

Every part of you is perfect.
Song of Songs 4:7

You are absolutely beautiful.
Song of Songs 4:1

I love you just the way you are.
Romans 8:38-39

When we spend time listening to what Jesus says about us, we will come away with lasting beauty. We'll be uplifted in our spirits and minds no matter if our hair is done, our nails are painted, or our makeup is perfect.

Agree with the One Who loves you. Speak the truth out loud:

- ♥ **Every part of me is perfect**
- ♥ **I am absolutely beautiful**
- ♥ **Jesus loves me just the way I am**

PRAYER: *Heavenly Father, thank You for making me beautiful and perfect in every part. Help me not to compare myself to other people and measure myself against them. I now know that I am perfect because of Jesus.*

STUDY QUESTIONS

Have you ever heard these lies?

LIES EXPOSED

You're not **beautiful**	_____ Yes	_____ No
You're not **perfect enough**	_____ Yes	_____ No
You **need** to change	_____ Yes	_____ No

How did these lies make you feel?

_____

_____

NOW LET'S STUDY THE TRUTH TOGETHER

Read **Song of Songs 7:1-7:**

[1]*"How beautiful are your sandaled feet, O queenly maiden. Your rounded thighs are like jewels, the work of a master craftsman.* [2]*Your navel is as delicious as a goblet filled with wine. Your belly is lovely...*[3]*Your breasts are like twin fawns of a gazelle.* [4]*Your neck is as stately as an ivory tower. Your eyes are like the sparkling pools...Your nose is as fine as the tower of Lebanon...* [5]*Your head is as majestic as Mount Carmel, and the sheen of your hair radiates royalty....* [6]*Oh, how delightful you are, my beloved, how pleasant for utter delight!* [7]*You are tall and slim like a palm tree...."*NLT

Fill in the blanks below. What does Jesus say about each part of you?

(v. 1) My feet are _____
My rounded thighs are like _____
(v. 2) My belly is _____
(v. 3) My breasts are like _____
(v. 4) My neck is as _____
My eyes are like _____
My nose is as _____
(v. 5) My head is as _____
The sheen of my hair _____
(v. 7) I am tall and _____ **like a palm tree.**

Look back at the **Song of Songs 7:1-7**. What does Jesus say about you in verse 6?

_____

_____

Read **Song of Songs 4:7**: *"You are so beautiful, my beloved, so perfect in every part."* NLT

What does Jesus say about every part of you?

_____

_____

Write **T** next to each statement that is true and **L** next to each one that is a lie:

____ I'm not perfect enough
____ I need to change
____ I'm not beautiful
____ I'm beautiful because of Jesus
____ Jesus loves me just the way I am
____ Every part of me is perfect

perfect

GOING DEEPER

TRUTH: I am perfect because of Jesus

What are some of the specific lies the devil says to you regarding being perfect?

_____

_____

What are the sources of most of these lies? (i.e., television, magazines)

_____

_____

Take a look at **Song of Songs 7:1-7** in your own Bible.

How did it make you feel, hearing Jesus speak these words of truth to your heart? _____

It's important to remember that what we listen to affects our heart. If television and magazines are the authority we go to for beauty, we will always have to change to meet today's standards. However, if what Jesus says is our standard, we know He always says the same thing to us and loves us just the way we are.

JOURNAL ENTRY

Write a short prayer to Jesus, asking Him to help you to continue to look only to Him to affirm your beauty and perfection:

_____

_____

What is the main truth that you learned from today's devotion?

_____

_____

Day 3
I Am Beautiful Within

Don't be concerned about the outward beauty that depends on fancy hairstyles, expensive jewelry, or beautiful clothes. You should be known for the beauty that comes from within, the unfading beauty of a gentle and quiet spirit, which is so precious to God. That is the way the holy women of old made themselves beautiful. They trusted God . . . . — *I Peter 3:3-5* NLT

In our last devotion you learned that Jesus thinks you're beautiful and perfect in every part and He has dressed you in His glory. He not only thinks you are beautiful on the outside, but beautiful on the inside as well. Whitney Thompson, the winner of *America's Next Top Model*, had this to say about beauty. "Beauty is acceptance. It's being kind to other people and accepting yourself."[7] Jaslene, another former winner, adds, "I vow to focus on what's on the inside, because inner beauty, peace, and happiness carry over into the beauty people see on the outside."[8]

If we look at the scripture above, we can see that beauty starts within our hearts. Jesus changes us from the inside out and our inner beauty shines for others to see. Our true beauty shines when we believe Jesus and let Him live His life through us.

When I was young, one of my most prized possessions was my musical jewelry box. It was simple, with a stem in back for winding the musical spring and a gold lock in front which only I could open with its key. Into its luxurious lining I placed my most valuable and precious treasures in the whole wide world: my April birthstone ring, a tiny golden cross and chain and an ID bracelet from my very first boyfriend. As I recall, the music box was simply decorated, so a quick glance gave no clue as to the wonders hidden inside. On many a lazy afternoon, I would wind it up, unlatch the lock with the key, and ever-so-slowly open the box. The tiny graceful ballerina would pop up and effortlessly twirl to the beautiful melody. One-by-one, I would lift each treasure from its place and reflect on its sweet memories; each representing parts of my life that were special to me. After daydreaming a while, I would neatly tuck my treasures back into their safe place, waiting for yet another day to reminisce.

Like my beautiful jewelry box was to me, your heart is precious to God, a place where He keeps His most priceless treasure stored. This treasure is Jesus who lives inside of you, and is revealed more and more as you look to Him and agree with what He says about you. In **1 John 4:17** the Bible tells us that we are just like Jesus, ***Because as He is, so are we in this world. AMP*** When you take on His opinion of you, you shine forth like a precious jewel to reflect His beauty.

Sometimes our true beauty does not shine forth because the devil brings sad, condemning thoughts to our hearts that don't allow God's light to shine. Have you ever heard these lies before:

You don't have a heart like Jesus
There's nothing good in You
You're not precious or valuable

The devil would like you to believe what he says instead of what Jesus says. But just like the holy women of old made themselves beautiful, as you trust in Jesus, you'll see His light shine forth in your life. Here are some of the truths Jesus wants you to remember...

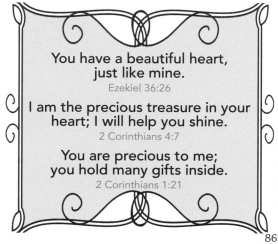

You have a beautiful heart, just like mine.
Ezekiel 36:26

I am the precious treasure in your heart; I will help you shine.
2 Corinthians 4:7

You are precious to me; you hold many gifts inside.
2 Corinthians 1:21

The beauty we hold within comes out as we agree with what Jesus says about us. As you look to Jesus and believe His words of love, the Holy Spirit will help your inner beauty shine. You will find yourself being loving and kind, full of joy and peace just like He is.

He'll do the work in you and you'll be like the ballerina in the music box, moving with His grace. The treasures of God will shine out of your heart effortlessly.

So agree with the One Who loves you and speak the truth out loud:

♥ **Jesus gave me a beautiful heart, just like His**

♥ **Jesus is the precious treasure in my heart; He will help me shine**

♥ **I am precious to Jesus; and I have many gifts inside**

PRAYER: *Heavenly Father, thank You for helping me to understand how precious I am to You, and that I hold a treasure in my heart – Jesus. Thank You that my heart is just like His and it shines like a jewel, reflecting His gifts of kindness, gentleness, peacefulness and joy for others to see. I know You love me and only speak the truth to me. Help me to believe what You say, so that my inner beauty will shine out for all to see.*

STUDY QUESTIONS

Have you ever believed these lies:

LIES EXPOSED

I don't **have** a **heart like Jesus** _____Yes _____ No

There's nothing good **in me** _____Yes _____ No

I'm not **precious** or **valuable** _____Yes _____ No

How did they make you feel?

NOW LET'S STUDY THE TRUTH TOGETHER

Read **1 Peter 3:3-5:** *Don't be concerned about the outward beauty that depends on fancy hairstyles, expensive jewelry, or beautiful clothes. You should be known for the beauty that comes from within, the unfading beauty of a gentle and quiet spirit, which is so precious to God. That is the way the holy women of old made themselves beautiful. They trusted God . . . . NLT*

What does this Scripture tell us not to be concerned with? Why?

_____

_____

What should we be known for that is precious to God?

_____

_____

How did the holy women of old make themselves beautiful?

_____

_____

Write **T** next to the statements that are true and **L** next to the ones that are lies:

_____ My beauty comes from my outward appearance

_____ I have a beautiful heart like Jesus

_____ There is nothing good in me

_____ I have the precious gifts of kindness, love, and peace in me

_____ Jesus lives in me; I am beautiful within

GOING DEEPER

TRUTH: I have a beautiful heart just like Jesus

The devil likes to lie to you and tell you that you don't have a heart like Jesus.

Read **Ezekiel 36:26** in your own Bible. What kind of heart did Jesus give you?

_____

Read **1 John 4:17**. Who are you like in this world?

_____

Read **Galatians 5:22-23**.

If you are like Jesus in this world, then what are His characteristics that you now have because He lives in you?

_____

_____

True beauty is the kindness, peace, joy, and love that Jesus has put in your heart. It shines forth when you trust Jesus and allow Him to love others through you.

Tell of a recent time when your inner beauty shone because of something kind you said or did for someone:

_____

_____

JOURNAL ENTRY:

The fruit that comes out in your life is directly related to what you believe about yourself. In your own words, write a prayer asking Jesus to help you believe Him so that your inner beauty can shine on those around you:

_____

_____

_____

_____

_____

What is the main truth that you learned from today's devotion?

_____

_____

_____

_____

_____

WEEK 5
THE COMPARISON TRAP
You're Valuable Because of Jesus
Connie Witter

Day 1
I Am Valuable

Day 2
I Am Special

Day 3
I Am Worthy of Love

Day 4
I Am Worth the Wait

♔
Day 1
I Am Valuable

For we are God's masterpiece. He has created us anew
in Christ Jesus.   — *Ephesians 2:10*

Have you ever been to visit a museum to see a beautiful work of art such as Leonardo da Vinci's famous painting, the *Mona Lisa*? Even if you don't know much about art, you've seen pictures of it in magazines and books because it's considered the greatest painting of all time, and a rare masterpiece. Regarded as priceless, its value today would be well over 500 million dollars. Can you imagine that a piece of canvas with some paint on it could be worth that much? The reason it is considered so valuable is because man placed a high value on it. Did you know that Jesus placed an even higher value on you? The value of something is determined by what someone is willing to pay for it; so let's take a look at how much Jesus was willing to pay for you. **1 Peter 1:18, 19** says, *You know that God paid a ransom to save you from the empty life you inherited from your ancestors. And the ransom He paid was not mere gold or silver. He paid for you with the precious lifeblood of Christ, the sinless, spotless Lamb of God.* NLT

Jesus proved that you were more valuable than His precious lifeblood because that is what He was willing to pay for you. *Valuable* means "expensive, precious, special, worthy and important."[9] According to Ephesians 2:10, you are God's masterpiece. You are priceless. The King of kings has declared you to be extremely valuable. You are expensive, precious, special, worthy and important because of Jesus.

Even though this is how God sees us, many of us don't feel very valuable because we seek our worth from something other than our relationship with Jesus. We base our value on our own opinion of ourselves or the world's opinion of us. When we allow the world to determine our value it causes us to suffer from low self-esteem and self-worth.

Have you ever compared yourself to others thinking your importance and value is based on:

> How you look?
> How many friends you have?
> What others think of you?
> How much you help others?
> How much money your family has?
> How well you do something?
> A position that you hold?
> A group you belong to?

When we base our value on these kinds of things, we fall right for the enemy's trap. It's called the "Comparison Trap," and it causes a broken place in our hearts. The enemy tries to get us to believe these lies:

I'm not as good as she is

I'm not as important as they are

I'm not as valuable as them

During junior high school, I often compared myself to the other girls by thinking things like, *Wow, she's much better at that than I am,* or *She is way more popular than me, Her family has more money than mine does,* or *She's prettier, smarter, and better dressed than me.*

Comparing myself to others only served to make me feel less valuable and important than others. I would often try to hide my insecurities by finding something I was better at than they were, but deep down it was because I really didn't think I measured up. Have you ever compared or tried to make yourself feel better in this same way?

It wasn't until years later that I began to understand the truth that has set my heart free from needing to compare myself to others. I came to see that I didn't need to base my value on the world's value rating system anymore. Instead, I could live in God's kingdom and allow the truth of what Jesus did for me determine my value and worth.

Jesus paid a great price to make you His own. Your value is not determined by how well you perform, a position that you hold, or whether you measure up to others, but rather on the fact that Jesus was willing to shed his precious blood for you. Listen to the wonderful truths He speaks to your heart...

When we believe what Jesus says about us, we can live confidently knowing that we are just as valuable, precious, and important as everyone else because of the great price He paid for us. You won't even think about comparing yourself to others any-more when you begin to understand just how valuable and precious you are to Jesus. So agree with Jesus, the One Who loves you.

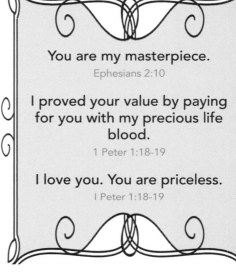

You are my masterpiece.
Ephesians 2:10

I proved your value by paying for you with my precious life blood.
1 Peter 1:18-19

I love you. You are priceless.
I Peter 1:18-19

Speak the truth out loud:

- ♥ **I am a masterpiece**
- ♥ **I am more valuable than the life blood of Jesus because that is what He was willing to pay for me**
- ♥ **I am loved by the King; I am priceless**

PRAYER: *Heavenly Father, thank You for showing me how valuable, precious and important I am to You because of the great price Jesus was willing to pay for me. There is no need for me to compare myself to others anymore; I can be happy and secure in the truth that I am valuable because I belong to You. I am Your masterpiece! Thank You for loving me so much!*

STUDY QUESTIONS

Have you ever fallen into the comparison trap and believed these lies?

LIES
EXPOSED

I'm not as good as she is   _____Yes _____ No

She is more important
than me   _____Yes _____ No

I'm not as valuable as she is _____Yes _____ No

How did you feel after you compared yourself to others?

_____

Read **2 Corinthians 10:12:** *When they measure themselves with themselves and compare themselves with one another, they are without understanding and behave unwisely.* AMP

Why do you think this verse tells us it is "unwise" to compare ourselves to others?

_____

_____

NOW LET'S STUDY THE TRUTH TOGETHER

Read **Ephesians 2:10:** *For we are God's masterpiece. He has created us anew in Christ Jesus.*

What are we called in this verse? Why does God think you're valuable?

_____

_____

Read **1 Peter 1:18, 19** again: *You know that God paid a ransom to save you from the empty life you inherited from your ancestors. And the ransom He paid was not mere gold and silver. He paid for you with the precious lifeblood of Christ, the sinless, spotless lamb of God.* NLT

What great price did Jesus pay for you? How does this prove that you are very valuable?

_____

_____

When we have extra money to spend it's fun to go shopping for new clothes. Yet, we wouldn't give our money for a piece of clothing if we didn't consider it more valuable than the money we had to pay for it. The same is true for Jesus. He wouldn't have given His precious life for you, if He didn't consider you more valuable than His precious life blood. How does it make your heart feel to realize that Jesus placed that much value on you? _____

_____

Write **T** next to the statements that are true and **L** next to the statements that are lies:

_____ I am not as good as some people

_____ My value is based on how well I do something

_____ I have to compare myself to others to see if I'm measuring up

_____ Everyone is important and valuable to God

_____ I am valuable because Jesus paid a great price for me

_____ I'm very important

GOING DEEPER

TRUTH: I am God's masterpiece

Read **Ephesians 2:10** again. Write down your immediate reaction to this truth:

_____

_____

_____

If you had difficulty believing it, what was the lie that immediately came to your mind?

_____

_____

_____

When you are tempted to determine your value by comparing yourself to others where can you turn to receive the truth about yourself? Write down what Jesus says about you that will help you overcome the devil's lies:

_____

_____

_____

JOURNAL ENTRY

Now write a prayer in your own words thanking Jesus for the great price that He paid for you, and that He thinks you are a masterpiece:

_____

_____

_____

_____

What is the main truth that you learned from today's devotion?

_____

_____

_____

_____

you are valuable

Day 2
I Am Special

But you are a chosen race, a royal priesthood, a dedicated nation, [God's] own purchased, special people.

— I Peter 2:9 AMP

Have you ever felt sad or uncomfortable thinking no one noticed you or that you weren't important or unique? God put in each of us the desire to be special and stand out in a crowd. That's why birthday parties are so much fun; we like getting all the attention and being celebrated just for being uniquely ourselves.

But even though we like attention, we don't always appreciate someone else getting it because it makes us feel insecure. The enemy often uses these times to whisper his lies into our ears:

You're not special

You'd get more attention if you were as important as they are

You're not loved as much as she is

As the middle child in a family of three children, I didn't feel very special. My sister was praised for being the model older child, and my brother got a lot of attention because he was the baby. Stuck in the middle, the devil would prey on my insecurities by whispering lies to my heart, like, *You don't even belong to this family. You're not special. Your sister is better than you. Your parents love your brother and sister more than they love you.* These thoughts plagued me, making my heart sad; I felt like I wasn't the favorite one.

Believing these lies, I grew up comparing myself to my sister, thinking she was better than me. It wasn't until I began to realize how much Jesus loved me that I really began to feel special.

In **Matthew 10:29-31** Jesus said, *"Not even a sparrow, worth only half a penny, can fall to the ground without your Father knowing it. And the very hairs on your head are all numbered. So don't be afraid; you are more valuable to him than a whole flock of sparrows."* NLT

Thinking on this scripture made me aware that my Heavenly Father does pay very special attention to me. If He's gone to the trouble of numbering the hairs on my head, I must be very valuable. Here's what He says to you and me . . .

> You are very special.
> 1 Peter 2:9
>
> I pay special attention to you.
> Matthew 10:29-31
>
> I have a special plan for your life.
> Psalm 139:14-18

The more I thought and began to believe these scriptures, the more loved and special I felt. The Bible tells us that God loves us the same way He loves Jesus. If Jesus is God's favorite Son, and Jesus lives inside of you, then you are God's favorite too! And God the Father has plenty of love to give, so we are all His favorites. You never have to worry that someone else is getting more attention than you. The Bible says you can't even count how many times a day your Heavenly Father thinks precious thoughts about you. You are unique and special to God and He wants you to feel especially loved!

So, agree with the One Who loves you. Speak the truth out loud:

- ♥ **I am very special**
- ♥ **Jesus pays special attention to me**
- ♥ **God has a special plan for my life; I am loved**

PRAYER: *Heavenly Father, thank You for showing me how very special I am to You, and that I don't have to be concerned about you caring for someone more than me. You purchased me with the blood of Your precious Son, Jesus, and You pay such close attention to me, that you've numbered every hair on my head. Your word tells me that you love me the same way you love Jesus, and because He lives inside of me, I am your favorite, too!*

STUDY QUESTIONS

Have you ever believed these lies:

LIES EXPOSED

I am not **special**	_____Yes	_____ No
They are more special than I am	_____Yes	_____ No
They are loved more than I am	_____Yes	_____ No

Why did you feel this way?

_____

_____

NOW LET'S STUDY THE TRUTH TOGETHER

Read **1 Peter 2:9** again: *But you are a chosen race, a royal priesthood, a dedicated nation, [God's] own purchased, special people.* AMP

What does this verse say about you?

_____

_____

You are special because of the price Jesus paid for you. Your Heavenly Father pays extra special attention to you.

Read **Matthew 10:29-31** again: *"Not even a sparrow worth only half a penny, can fall to the ground without your Father knowing it. And the very hairs on your head are all numbered. So don't be afraid; you are more valuable to him than a whole flock of sparrows."* NLT

What did Jesus say about you in these verses? Why are you special?

_____

_____

_____

Write **T** next to the statements that are true and **L** next to the ones that are lies:

_____ I am not very special
_____ No one pays attention to me
_____ I am God's own purchased, special daughter
_____ Jesus pays special attention to me
_____ I am very loved
_____ God has a special plan for my life

GOING DEEPER

TRUTH: Jesus thinks I'm special

Read **Psalm 139: 1-18.** What do these verses say about how special you are to God and the special attention He gives to you? Write down some truths you learned from this passage of Scripture:

_____

_____

_____

_____

JOURNAL ENTRY

Write a prayer in your own words, thanking God for making you special:

_____

_____

_____

_____

What is the main truth that you learned from today's devotion?

_____

_____

_____

_____

Day 3
I Am Worthy of Love

God showed his great love for us by sending Christ to die for us while we were still sinners. — Romans 5:8

Jesus proved that you are worthy of love by laying His life down for you. You are the apple of His eye, His most precious possession. You are valuable and special to Him.

The devil doesn't want you to believe that you are worthy of love, so he uses any opportunity he can to make you feel unworthy. Have you ever had someone call you a bad name or treat you in an unkind way? Hurtful words sadden our hearts and may make us wonder if what was said was true. They may cause us to question our worth. The devil uses these opportunities to try and get us to believe these lies:

You are not worthy of love

You are no good; You deserve to be treated badly

What they said about you is true

When we allow people to treat us badly it's because we really don't see ourselves as valuable. But Jesus said to return good for evil, which means that when someone treats us wrong we can look to Jesus for the power to pray for them and to be kind to them in spite of the hurtful things that were said. This doesn't mean, however, that we have to hang out with people who continually make us feel bad.

Recently, one of my daughters had a friend who was continually treating her badly, saying unkind things and ignoring her. Because my daughter desired her friendship, she put up with this behavior for a while. As my daughter realized that she was valuable to Jesus and worthy to be treated with love and respect, she saw that she didn't have to fear losing this friendship because Jesus would bring other friends into her life that would treat her right. So, we prayed together and asked Jesus to give her the courage to talk to her friend about the situation.

After being treated badly once again, my daughter had an opportunity to speak to her friend. "I am a good friend," my daughter confidently said, "and I don't deserve to be treated with disrespect. I do want to hang out with you, but I won't if you continue to treat me this way. So, you decide whether you want to be my friend or not, because I still want to be yours." Not realizing the effect her actions had caused, her friend told her she was sorry and began to treat her better.

Later on as my daughter shared what had happened, she said she felt Jesus giving her the courage to talk to her friend. She wasn't mean, but valued herself enough to speak the truth of what Jesus had said about her and refused to be treated with disrespect. Although she wanted this girl's friendship, she didn't need it if it wasn't the kind of friendship that Jesus would want for her.

Jesus is always there to remind you of how valuable you are. When someone says something hurtful to you or treats you wrong, remember what Jesus has to say....

You are worthy of love and respect.
Romans 5:8

You are the apple of my eye.
Zechariah 2:8

You are my most treasured possession.
Psalm 135:4

As you believe the truth, you'll find yourself being more and more confident that you are worthy of love and respect. The next time someone says something hurtful to you, you'll stand up boldly and say, "That is not true about me."

God will give you the courage to walk away from any unhealthy relationship in your life. When you believe that you are worthy of love, you'll choose friends that treat you well. Jesus wants you to surround yourself with people who will encourage you, and treat you well because you are valuable and very precious to Him.

So, agree with the One Who loves you. Speak the truth out loud:

♥ **I am worthy of love**

♥ **I am the apple of God's eye**

♥ **Jesus loves me; I'm His most treasured possession**

PRAYER: *Heavenly Father, thank You so much for showing me how valuable I am to You and worthy of Your love. I know You want me to have friends that are kind and encouraging, who treat me with dignity and respect. Help me to pray for those I meet that don't treat me well, and give me the courage to walk away from relationships that are not good. Thank You for showing me how valuable I am, that I am the "apple of your eye," precious to you and worthy of love!*

STUDY QUESTIONS

Have you ever heard these lies in your heart?

LIES EXPOSED

You're not worthy of love	____ Yes	____ No
You deserve to be treated badly	____ Yes	____ No
What they said about you is true	____ Yes	____ No

Have you ever had someone treat you badly? How did it make you feel?

_____

_____

NOW LET'S STUDY THE TRUTH TOGETHER

Read **Zechariah 2:8:** *For this is what the LORD Almighty says… "for whoever touches you touches the apple of his eye." NIV*

The expression *apple of His eye*,[10] means that you are the center of God's attention and most important to Him. You are God's treasured possession.

Read **Romans 5:8**: *"God showed his great love for us by sending Christ to die for us while we were still sinners."*

How did Jesus prove that you are valuable and worthy of love?

_____

_____

Write **T** next to the statements that are true and **L** next to the ones that are lies:

_____ I am not worthy of love

_____ I deserve to be treated badly

_____ Those negative words are true about me

_____ I am worthy of love and respect

_____ I am valuable, special, and precious because of Jesus

_____ Jesus wants me to have friends that are
         kind and encouraging

GOING DEEPER

TRUTH: **Jesus proved that I'm worthy of love!**

Read **Ephesians 4:29, 32** in your own Bible.

Explain the kind of relationships Jesus wants you to have. How does He want us to treat each other?

_____

_____

Is there a person in your life right now who is not treating you right? What did you learn from the story in today's devotion about how to handle a person in your life who is not treating you with kindness?

_____

_____

_____

JOURNAL ENTRY:

Write a prayer in your own words, thanking Jesus for making you worthy of His love:

_____

_____

_____

_____

_____

What is the main truth that you learned from today's devotion?

_____

_____

_____

_____

Jesus made you worthy of love!

Day 4
I Am Worth the Wait

Shun immorality and all sexual looseness…. Do you not know that your body is the temple (the very sanctuary) of the Holy Spirit Who lives within you, Whom you have received [as a Gift] from God? You are not your own, you were bought with a price [purchased with a preciousness and paid for, made His own]. So then, honor God and bring glory to Him in your body. — I Corinthians 6:18-20 AMP

Your body was purchased with the precious blood of Jesus. God created you holy, pure and beautiful. Your body is a precious treasure box, only to be discovered and opened by your prince — the man you will marry. It is God's design for the mystery of your beauty to be revealed on your wedding day to the man who loves you and has chosen you to be his bride. You're a genuine princess and you are worth the wait.

Song of Songs 4:12 says, *"You are like a private garden, my treasure, my bride! You are like a spring that no one else can drink from, a fountain of my own."* NLT

Solomon described his beloved's body as a private garden that no one else can drink from. This refers to her virginity. It is a treasure she will share only with her husband.

The world sees no value in a young girl's virginity. You can tell by the movies and magazines that the world sees a girl as something a man uses for his own pleasure and then when he's done, he moves on to someone else. The devil tries his best to get young girl's to believe that it's okay to share her garden with anyone. The devil knows this will bring shame and heartache into her life and cause a princess to feel unworthy and devalued. And that is exactly his evil plan.

When I was sixteen, I began dating a boy who eventually became my husband. As a young Christian girl, I had determined in my heart that I would wait until marriage to become intimate with a man, but over the course of several months, the devil began his work on my heart and deceived me with these lies:

Everyone else is doing it so it must be okay

Its okay if you're in love

The world's way looks more fun

Believing the devil's lies, I gave away the precious gift God gave me to give as a wedding present to my husband. I became pregnant before I was married and felt in my heart that I was an embarrassment to my parents. This caused me great shame and heartache and the devil continued to throw these fiery lies at my heart, *You'll never be happy because you disobeyed God. You have to pay for your mistake for the rest of your life. You deserve to have a hard life.* Oh, how I wished I could turn back time and get a second chance, but that was impossible. My only hope was found in Jesus and His forgiveness and grace.

When I turned to Him with my broken heart, I heard Him speak these words of love....

Jesus doesn't want you to go through the heartache and pain of giving away your private garden to anyone other than your husband. Your virginity is a special gift that a husband and wife give to each other on their wedding day. You are a precious treasure, a princess in God's kingdom and you are worth the wait.

But if for some reason, like me, you have let someone in, know that you are

> **You are my precious treasure.**
> I Corinthians 6:18-20
>
> **I don't even remember your mistakes.**
> Hebrews 8:12
>
> **You are justified. You are pure and holy in my sight.**
> Jude 1:24

cleansed by the precious blood of Jesus. *Justified* means that it is "just-as-if-I'd" done everything right in God's sight.[11] His forgiveness and grace are new every morning. As you keep your eyes on Jesus, He will empower you to believe the truth and value yourself enough to keep yourself pure until your wedding day. So agree with the one who loves you:

♥ **I am a precious treasure and I am worth the wait**

♥ **I am pure and holy because of Jesus**

♥ **My body is a gift to my husband on our wedding day**

PRAYER: *Heavenly Father, thank You for showing me that my body is a precious treasure and it was designed by You to be a wedding gift to my husband. Give me the strength not to believe the lies of the devil and not to follow the world's way instead of Yours. I want to live in Your kingdom. I want to glorify and honor You with my body. I know that Your grace is sufficient for me.*

STUDY QUESTIONS

Have you ever heard the devil speak these lies to your heart:

LIES EXPOSED

Everyone else is doing it so it must be okay   _____Yes _____ No

It's okay **if you love someone**   _____Yes _____ No

The world's way looks more fun   _____Yes _____ No

Why do you think the devil wants you to believe his lies?

_____

_____

NOW LET'S STUDY THE TRUTH TOGETHER

Read **1 Corinthians 6:18-20**: *Shun immorality and all sexual looseness.... Do you not know that your body is the temple (the very sanctuary) of the Holy Spirit Who lives within you, Whom you have received [as a Gift] from God? You are not your own, you were bought with a price [purchased with a preciousness and paid for, made His own]. So then, honor God and bring glory to Him in your body.* AMP

Why are you worth the wait? How can you glorify God in your body?

_____

_____

Write **T** next to the statements that are true, and
L next to the ones that are lies:

_____ Everyone else is doing it so it must be okay

_____ I am not valuable

_____ The world's way will make me happy

_____ I am pure and holy because of Jesus!

_____ My body is like a treasure box that is only
to be opened by my husband

_____ I am worth the wait

GOING DEEPER

TRUTH: **I am valuable and I am worth the wait**

Read **1 Corinthians 6:11-18** in your own Bible.

Write down the truths you discovered in each verse.

Verse 11:_____

Verse 13:_____

Verse 17:_____

Verse 18:_____

Verses 19 & 20_____

_____

What lies has the devil tried to get you to believe about your virginity?

_____

_____

_____

What truth have you chosen to believe today?

JOURNAL ENTRY

Talk to Jesus about what you learned today. Ask Him for the grace to keep yourself pure.

What is the main truth you learned from today's devotion?

Jesus made you worth the wait!

WEEK 6

BEST FRIENDS FOREVER

You're Accepted Because of Jesus

Connie Witter

Day 1
I Am Accepted

Day 2
I Am Approved

Day 3
I Am Favored

Day 1
I Am Accepted

He hath made us accepted in the beloved. — *Ephesians 1:6* KJV

This Scripture tells us that Jesus made us "accepted in the beloved," which means that because of what He has done for you, you are totally accepted by your Heavenly Father. The word *accepted* means "chosen, approved, and favored."[12] When you are accepted by someone it means that they desire your friendship and really want you to be a part of their life.

God put the need for friendship in each of our hearts. All of our lives we

search for acceptance by someone. When I was in high school, I was on the dance team. I remember all the drama that went on between the girls. Each of us just wanted to be accepted, but jealousy, gossip, and rejection was a common occurrence. On one particular day at school, several girls who were supposed to be my friends, were mad at me. I didn't even know what I did wrong. I heard the mean things they were saying behind my back. It was a lot like the plot in the movie, *Mean Girls*.

The devil used this opportunity to throw his fiery darts at my heart. Have you had a similar experience and heard these lies before:

There's something wrong with you!

You're not good enough!

You're a reject!

During this time in my life, I found myself worried about what people were saying about me and whether or not they would accept me and want to be my friend. There were days that I didn't even want to go to school because I didn't want to deal with rejection. Have you ever feared not being accepted by a group of people? The fear of rejection is something we all face as girls and even as grown women. It causes us to pull away from relationships with others for fear that we will be hurt by them. The devil wants us to believe that we are rejected. I used to believe this lie until I realized how much Jesus loved me and began to believe what He said about me.

The Good News is that Jesus was rejected for you and me so that we could be completely accepted. When Jesus died on the cross for you, He took your rejection, and the punishment you would have received for all the wrong things you've done. He did this so that you could be accepted by the Father and receive all of His blessings.

Jesus wants you to have godly friends, but most importantly, He wants to be your best friend. You don't ever have to fear being rejected because the truth is that you are accepted in Him. He'll never reject you, never turn His back on you, and never talk bad about you. You can share your heart with Him, and He'll always love and accept you no matter what you say or do. He is your best friend forever and this is what He always says about you…

There are still times in my life when people reject me, but now I know that I can turn to Jesus and talk to Him about any hurt I may feel in my heart. He always reminds me of truth of who I am in Him and my heart is made whole with His words of love. He gives me the power to love others without fear of rejection because I know I am completely accepted in Him.

You are good enough.
2 Corinthians 5:21

You are my best friend.
John 15:13

You are loved and accepted by Me.
Ephesians 1:6

When you believe what Jesus says about you, you, too, will live free from the fear of rejection. You'll be completely confident in the truth that you are accepted by the most important person in the whole world, your Heavenly Father, the King of kings. You're a genuine princess. You can be friendly to those around you and if they don't like you, that's okay, because Jesus has met the need within your heart to feel accepted. You can be confident in His great love!

115

So agree with the One Who loves you! Speak the truth out loud:

- ♥ **Because of Jesus, I am good enough**
- ♥ **Jesus is my best friend**
- ♥ **I am loved and accepted by Him**

PRAYER: *Heavenly Father, thank You for loving and accepting me. I choose to believe what You say about me, that I am accepted in Jesus. I don't need to be concerned about whether I am accepted by others or not. When I believe the truth it makes my heart happy. I know I am loved by You and that is what makes me able to love others with Your amazing love!*

STUDY QUESTIONS

Have you ever heard the devil speak these lies to your heart:

There's something wrong with you _____Yes _____ No

You're not good enough _____Yes _____ No

You're a reject _____Yes _____ No

Why do you think the devil wants you to believe these lies?

_____

_____

NOW LET'S STUDY THE TRUTH TOGETHER

Read **Ephesians 1:6:** *To the praise of the glory of his grace, wherein he hath made us <u>accepted</u> in the beloved.* **KJV**

What does this Scripture say about you?

_____

_____

What does it mean to be accepted by Jesus? Read the first paragraph of your devotion again to find the answer:

_____

_____

Read John 15:15. What does Jesus call you?

_____

Write **T** next to the statements that are true, and **L** next to the ones that are lies:

_____ I'm rejected

_____ Something's wrong with me

_____ I'm not good enough

_____ I am loved and accepted

_____ Jesus calls me His friend

_____ Jesus made me good enough; I am righteous in Him

GOING DEEPER

TRUTH: I am accepted in Jesus

Read **Isaiah 53:3-12** in your own Bible.

What happened to Jesus so that you could be forgiven and accepted as righteous in God's sight? Write two words or phrases on each line that describe what happened to Him:

Verse 3: _____

Verse 5: _____

Verse 7: _____

Verse 9: _____

What did Jesus make possible by going through such rejection?

Verse 11: _____

The word *justify* in verse 11 means that Jesus took away all your sins and made you righteous. *Righteous* means that you stand perfect before God without a single fault; that there is nothing wrong with you. Jesus made you good enough. How does knowing that make you feel?

_____

Have you ever had the experience of being rejected by someone? How did that make your heart feel?

_____

_____

What lie did the devil get you to believe as a result of this situation?

_____

_____

If you experience rejection by someone again, how will you handle the situation differently now that you know the truth of who you are in Jesus: _____

_____

JOURNAL ENTRY

Take time to write a prayer from your heart about what you learned today. You may even need to talk to Jesus about a particular hurtful situation that you are dealing with right now in your life. Remember, He is your best friend! _____

_____

_____

_____

What is the main truth that you learned from today's devotion?

_____

_____

_____

Day 2
I Am Approved

Before I formed you in the womb, I knew you and approved of you.
— Jeremiah 1:5 AMP

This Scripture says that even before you were born, and before you were able to do anything right or anything wrong, your Heavenly Father approved of you. The word *approve* means "to have or express a favorable opinion of someone and to be very pleased with them."[13] When your Heavenly Father thinks of you, you make Him smile. He always has a good opinion of you. He's very pleased with you not because you've done everything right, but because you believe in Jesus.

Have you ever found yourself worrying about someone's opinion of you? We all want to do things right so that we get other people's approval. At the same time, and in spite of our best efforts, we sometimes make mistakes. We have all experienced that disapproving look that causes us to think, *They are not happy with me. I've done something to upset them.* We've all experienced disapproval from our parents, teachers and friends. This may cause us to believe that when we do something wrong, God disapproves of us too. Have you ever heard these lies in your head:

God disapproves of you
He is angry with you
You'll never be good enough to make God happy

The truth is that because of Jesus, you will always have your Heavenly Father's approval. He'll never change His good opinion of you. He promises that He'll never be angry with you or rebuke you. He says...

I approve of you.
Jeremiah 1:5
I will never be angry with you.
Isaiah 54:9,10
My good opinion of you will never change because you are in Jesus.
Ephesians 1:4

119

Jesus showed us how the Father looks at us when we do wrong through a parable in the Bible called the "Prodigal Son." In **Luke 15:11-24**, Jesus told this story of a Father whose youngest son wanted his inheritance so he could leave their family's home. So, the Father gave him a very large sum of money, and the boy went on his way. After spending his inheritance on sinful living which brought sadness to his heart, he found himself, poor, sad, and rejected by everyone, living in a pigpen. Being hungry, he knew that his father's hired servants were eating better than him, so he made a plan to go home. Since he thought his Father might be angry with Him and reject him because of his bad behavior, he rehearsed what he would say, "Father, I have sinned! I don't deserve your blessing or to be called your son, but please just let me be your servant."

When the Father saw his son walking toward his home, his response was different than the boy had imagined. Instead of being angry, He was overjoyed that his son had returned, and he ran to him, hugging him around the neck and kissing him over and over. The Father's heart was filled only with love and compassion for the son he had missed.

As the boy began his rehearsed speech, "Father, I'm not worthy of your approval, I have been bad, I have disappointed you," the Father stopped him from finishing, and said to the servants, "Put a robe on my son, a ring on his finger, sandals on his feet, and kill a calf to eat. My son who was lost has come back home and we are going to celebrate!"

Jesus told this story to help us understand how our Heavenly Father feels toward us when we've done wrong. When Your Heavenly Father looks at you, His heart is filled with love and compassion for you. He doesn't want you to sin because He knows that it will bring sadness into your life, but it does not change the way He feels about you. He will always love and approve of you.

The point is, you don't have to look to others anymore to feel approved. In fact, in **John 5:41**, Jesus said to a group of people, *"Your approval [or disapproval] means nothing to me."**Jesus didn't need the approval of men, because He already knew He had the approval of His Father, which would never change. The Good News is that Your Heavenly Father approves of you, too, just like He does Jesus. So the next time you feel

*Author's emphasis

like someone disapproves of you, look to Jesus, your best friend, and agree with the One Who loves you. Speak the truth out loud:

- ♥ **My Heavenly Father approves of me**
- ♥ **He will never be angry with me**
- ♥ **His good opinion of me will never change because of Jesus**

PRAYER: *Heavenly Father, thank You for loving me even when I do things that are wrong. You approve of me because Jesus took away all my sins and made me perfect in Your sight. You favor me and Your good opinion of me never changes. When I agree with what You say about me, it makes me happy and fills my heart with joy! I feel so blessed to be loved by You!*

STUDY QUESTIONS

Have you ever heard the devil speak these lies to your heart:

God does not approve
of you   _____Yes _____ No

God is angry
with you   _____Yes _____ No

You'll never be good enough
to make God happy _____Yes _____ No

Why did you think that God might not be happy with you?

_____

_____

_____

NOW, LET'S STUDY THE TRUTH TOGETHER

Read **Jeremiah 1:5:** *Before I formed you in the womb I knew [and] approved of you.* AMP

How does this truth make your heart feel?

_____

_____

Mark **T** next to the statements that are true and **L** next to the ones that are lies:

_____ My Heavenly Father is pleased with me
because I believe in Jesus
_____ I have to try harder if I want to please God
_____ Sin will bring sadness into my life
_____ When I do wrong, my Heavenly Father is angry with me
_____ My Heavenly Father will never be angry with me
because of Jesus

GOING DEEPER

TRUTH: **My Heavenly Father approves of me**

Read **Isaiah 54:9-10** in your own Bible.

Even when you do something wrong, what did God promise He would never feel toward you?

_____

What did He say He would always feel toward you?

_____

_____

There are some stories in the Old Testament that tell us that God was angry at people because of their sin, but the Bible says that Jesus died on the cross for your sins. He took the punishment and anger that you deserved upon Himself so that you could be free to receive God's love and blessing. In the New Covenant God promises that He'll never be angry with you again even when you do something wrong.

Read **Luke 15:11-24** in your own Bible.

Verse 14: What happened to the son when he lived a life of sin?

_____

When he approached his father after he'd done wrong, how did his father feel toward him?

_____

_____

What does this story teach you about how your Heavenly Father feels toward you when you come to him after you have done wrong?

_____

_____

JOURNAL ENTRY

Write a prayer in your own words about what you learned today:

_____

_____

_____

_____

_____

What is the main truth you learned from today's devotion?

_____

_____

_____

_____

Day 3
I Am Favored

For surely, O LORD, you bless the righteous; you surround them
with your favor as with a shield. — *Psalm 5:12 NIV*

Jesus has made you righteous. We learned in an earlier devotion that this means that God has made us good and perfect in His sight. The above verse explains that because you are righteous, the Lord will bless you with *favor*, which means "a friendly regard shown toward another [person] or a gracious act of kindness." [14] Because Jesus has made you righteous, God will cause others to look upon you favorably, and treat you like a friend.

Part of your Heavenly Father's plan for your life includes godly friends. As you believe what He says about you — that you are favored — He will bless your life with favor and surround you with wonderful godly friends.

God put in all of us the need and desire to have friends. In **Proverbs 18:24**, the Bible says, ***A man that hath friends must show himself friendly. KJV*** But sometimes it's hard to make friends with someone you don't know, especially when the devil is whispering his lies in your ears. These are some of his lies which can keep us from making new friends:

You don't know how to make new friends

They're not going to like you

They aren't interested in what you have to say

For a long time, I believed these lies and they made me feel uncomfortable around new people. I didn't know what to say and thought they might not like me. Have you ever been afraid to meet new people?

Then I learned the truth of what Jesus said about me. I began to listen to His words of love toward me. This is what Jesus says to me, and to you, too...

When I began to think upon what Jesus said, it made my heart happy, and I began to believe that people did like me. Then God filled my life with wonderful, loving friends just like He promised. And as I looked to Him, He showed me how to be a good friend; how to talk and act like a friend.

God didn't promise that everyone would like us, but He did say He would surround us with people who do. When we believe Him, He'll help us to be confident and friendly around others, and He will surround us with godly friends. So the next time you're tempted to draw back and be shy around new people, remember to look to Jesus and believe what He says about you.

> **I will bless you with godly friends.**
> Luke 2:52
>
> **I will surround you with favor.**
> Psalm 5:12
>
> **I will show you what to say.**
> Jeremiah 1:9

So, agree with the One Who loves you. Say these truths out loud:

- ♥ **I am blessed and favored because of Jesus**
- ♥ **God surrounds me with godly friends**
- ♥ **Because Jesus loves me, He shows me what to say**

PRAYER: *Heavenly Father, thank You for surrounding me with favor. I ask You to bring godly friends into my life. Help me to believe what You say about me when I'm tempted to believe that people won't like me. I can be confident and friendly around new people because I have favor. I am blessed because of Jesus!*

STUDY QUESTIONS

Have you ever believed these lies:

LIES EXPOSED

They won't like me	_____ Yes	_____ No
They aren't interested in what I have to say	_____ Yes	_____ No
I don't know what to say	_____ Yes	_____ No

How did it affect the way you felt when you were around new people?

_____

_____

_____

NOW LET'S STUDY THE TRUTH TOGETHER

Read **Psalm 5:12**. Jesus made you righteous. What does your Heavenly Father say about you in this verse?

_____

_____

Read **1 John 4:16-19**: Fill in the blanks below:

Verse 16: **And we have come to know and** _____ **the love God has for us.**

Verse 17: **As Jesus is, so are we in this** _____

Verse 18: **Perfect love casts out** _____

Have you ever been afraid to meet new people? _____ Yes _____ No
Why were you afraid?

_____

_____

_____

The Bible says that when we know and believe the love of God, we won't be afraid of anything. His perfect love frees us from all fear when we believe the truth of what Jesus says about us.

Verse 17 said that you are just like Jesus in this world.

Read **Luke 2:52**. What was Jesus blessed with as he grew up in the world?

_____

If you are just like Him, what are you blessed with as you grow up in the world?

_____

Mark **T** next to the statements that are true and **L** next to the statements that are lies:

_____ I should be afraid that people aren't going to like me
_____ I'm just like Jesus, I have favor with God and man
_____ My Heavenly Father surrounds me with godly friends
_____ People aren't interested in what I have to say
_____ I am blessed and favored because of Jesus!

GOING DEEPER

TRUTH: Jesus is my Best Friend

Read **James 2:23**: *And so it happened just as the Scriptures say: "Abraham believed God, and God counted him as righteous because of his faith." He was even called the friend of God.*

According to the above scripture, what did Abraham do to be counted as righteous?

_____

_____

Because Abraham believed God, what did God call him?

_____

_____

Isn't it amazing, that just like Abraham, when you believe God, He calls you His friend! How does it make you feel to realize that Jesus is your best friend forever?

_____

_____

_____

_____

_____

JOURNAL ENTRY

Now, in your own words, write a prayer asking God to help you believe what He says about you:

_____

_____

_____

_____

_____

What is the main truth that you learned from today's devotion?

_____

_____

_____

_____

_____

are accepted

approved

you are favored

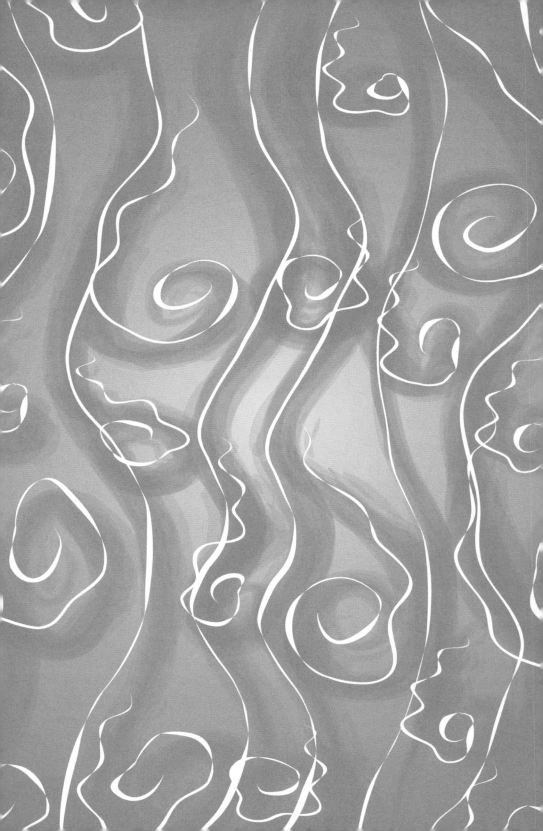

WEEK 7

AMERICAN IDOL
You're Wonderful
Because of Jesus
Rose Karlebach

Day 1
I Am Wonderful

Day 2
I Am Adored

Day 3
I Am Gifted

Day 1
I Am Wonderful

I praise you because you made me in an amazing and wonderful way. What you have done is wonderful. I know this very well.
— *Psalm 139:14 NCV*

Were you aware that God thinks that you are wonderful just because He made you? His opinion is not based on anything you do, but on what Jesus has done for you. The Good News is that God's opinion about you will never change. Unfortunately, that's not how the rest of the world thinks, and in a flash someone's opinion of you can go from good to bad. Take *American Idol*, for instance. Each week my family and I watch as a group of young singers compete to win the title of "American Idol" and a recording contract and tour. We grow to love the singers, getting more excited as our favorite ones move closer to winning the grand prize.

But just as important as the singing are the opinions of the judges, all experts in the music industry. After each song, all eyes in TV land turn to the judges hoping to hear, "You were fantastic!" "Wonderful!" "Amazing!" or "Best of the night!" We're so excited when our favorites get a good response! But our hearts sink with them when we hear things like, "You were awful," "That was a disappointment," or "That was a really bad performance!" We want the judges to say something nice, no matter how badly the singers have performed.

As I've watched the program, I sometimes think that the devil would love to be a judge on the show! The truth is you don't even have to be in a singing competition to hear his negative opinions:

> You are awful
>
> You are a disappointment
>
> You are bad

As a teenager, I got tired of being considered a "goody-two-shoes." Wanting to be cool, I decided to stay out late one night and go to a party with a group of kids. Well, word got out, and the next day several adults I respected called to tell me that "What I had done was awful," that "I was a disappointment to them," and worst of all, that "I was a bad person." Wow! In one night, because of my poor judgment, I went from being a good person, to a bad one, and that devastated me for a long time.

Just like the singers on *American Idol*, we can all have an off day, a bad performance, or a lapse in judgment, and we've all had negative opinions spoken over us as a result. It was not until I began to understand what God's opinion of me was that my heart began to heal. That's why **Psalm 139:14** is so encouraging. It says that Our Heavenly Father — who is greater than all of the *American Idol* judges rolled into one! — thinks we're *wonderful*, which means "excellent, great, marvelous; amazing, astonishing."[15] And it's not based on our performance, but on Jesus' performance, which by the way, was perfect! Because Jesus lives inside of us, when the Father looks at us, this is His opinion…

You are very good.
Psalm 139:14

You are excellent and amazing.
Psalm 139:14

You are wonderful.
Psalm 139:14

Now that I know what Jesus thinks about me, I'm free to be myself no matter what anyone else thinks. And I don't have to be overly worried about my performance because when I do good, it's as if Jesus is performing inside of me and He does everything perfect. On top of that, if I slip, or make a mistake I know I can turn back to Jesus for help and restoration because He thinks I'm good, and He'll give me the power to be good. The Good News is I can watch *American Idol* in peace, knowing that the greatest judge of them all thinks I'm wonderful!

So believe what Jesus says about you and agree with the one who loves you. Speak the truth out loud:

- ♥ **I am very good**
- ♥ **My Heavenly Father thinks I'm excellent and amazing**
- ♥ **I am wonderful because of Jesus**

PRAYER: *Thank You, Lord, that You don't judge me based on my performance, but on Jesus and His performance was perfect. Remind me that even if I make a mistake, You still think that I am good. Thank You so much that You think I am wonderful, amazing and marvelous because of Jesus. And help me to believe this truth no matter what others' opinions of me may be.*

STUDY QUESTIONS

Have you ever heard the devil speak these lies to your heart:

You're awful	_____Yes	_____ No
You are a disappointment	_____Yes	_____ No
You are bad	_____Yes	_____ No

LIES EXPOSED

How did these lies make you feel?

_____

_____

_____

NOW LET'S STUDY THE TRUTH TOGETHER

Psalm 139:13-14 says: *¹³For you created my inmost being; you knit me together in my mother's womb. ¹⁴I praise you because I am fearfully and wonderfully made; your works are wonderful, I know that full well.* NIV

Look at verse 13. Who created you?

_____

Read verse 14 again. How were you made? And what does that mean in your own words?

_____

_____

Go back and read the fifth paragraph of this devotion. Look at the definition of *wonderful* again. Fill in the blanks with the words that describe how Jesus made you.

I am _____, _____,

_____, _____,

and_____ because of Jesus!

Write **T** next to the statements that are true, and next to the ones that are lies.

_____ Jesus made me wonderful!

_____ I have to perform perfectly for God to love me

_____ I'm bad

_____ I need to believe people's negative opinions of me.

_____ Jesus performed perfectly on my behalf

_____ God the Father thinks I'm very good!

GOING DEEPER

TRUTH: Jesus thinks I'm wonderful

The opposite of *wonderful* is *awful,* which means "extremely bad, unpleasant, terrible."[16] Has the devil ever used these words against you or against something that you have done? How did it make you feel?

_____

_____

_____

Read Psalm 139:13-18 in your Bible.

How will you respond differently the next time the devil tries to make you feel bad about yourself? What does Jesus say about you?

_____

_____

_____

JOURNAL ENTRY

Write a prayer in your own words about what you learned today:

_____

_____

_____

_____

_____

What is the main truth you learned from today's devotion?

_____

_____

_____

_____

_____

👑
Day 2
I Am Adored

The LORD your God is in the midst of you, a Mighty One, a Savior [Who saves]! He will rejoice over you with joy; He will rest [in silent satisfaction] and in His love He will be silent and make no mention [of past sins, or even recall them], He will exult over you with singing.
— Zephaniah 3:17 AMP

Isn't it something to know that Your Heavenly Father adores you and He rejoices over you with singing? Do you know why He adores you so much? It's because you have placed your faith in Jesus and it makes His heart so happy. As a matter of fact, Luke 15:7 says the day you asked Jesus into your heart, all of heaven rejoiced over you!

Jesus is your biggest fan! If you've been watching *American Idol*, or any of the reality programs like it, you can't help but notice all the adoring fans of the performers out in the audience. Some of them hold up huge photos of the contestants or giant banners that read, "We Love You!" We admire the fact that the performers are so adored by their fans. It warms our hearts; we all want to be adored!

The word *adore* means "to regard with the utmost esteem, love, respect; and honor. To like or admire very much."[17] God put the desire to be adored in all of us. But we think that the key to our happiness is to have adoring fans, wealth and fame like these performers do. The truth is, those things are no guarantee of happiness. Some of the richest and most famous people in the world have led the saddest lives even though they had millions of fans. You see, the devil wants to trick us into feeling that we can only be happy if we have lots of adoring fans. Because of that, he fills our ears with these lies:

You **will** only **be adored if** you **are rich** and **famous**

No one admires you   No one adores you

I remember as a teenager, believing these very same lies. I didn't like myself very much, and I thought that the love of adoring fans would fill the empty hole inside of my heart. So, I moved to New York to take acting lessons and study performing. But no matter how many scenes I performed, how well I performed them, or the applause I got, it did not really convince me that I was adored. It only made the hole in my heart bigger, because I did not believe what anyone said. The problem was that I did not love myself because I didn't know how much God loved me.

That's why scriptures like **Zephaniah 3:17** really changed my life. In it, Jesus is telling us that we are adored, and it's not because we are rich and famous, but just because He loves us and is pleased that we have placed our faith in what Jesus has done for us. He took away all our sins and made us righteous and perfect in the Father's sight. This scripture is telling us that Jesus is our greatest fan, in fact, He's the President of our fan club! It says, *He will exult over you with singing*. The word *exult* means, "to show or feel a lively triumphant joy, to rejoice exceedingly, to leap for joy, to delight in."[18] Jesus delights over you and you give Him great joy! And it's not because you "perform" for Him, it's just because He thinks you're so wonderful! In fact, He's so happy with you, that you don't even have to perform, you can sit back and remember that He is singing over you just because He loves you! I remember as a young girl, watching movies where the handsome prince sang to the princess, and that is exactly what this scripture says Jesus is doing over you. As an added bonus, all those mistakes you've ever made, well guess what? Your handsome Prince paid the price for them, and He doesn't even remember they ever happened! He just wants to sit with you and love you.

I delight in you.
Zephaniah 3:17

I rejoice over you with singing
You make my heart happy.
Zephaniah 3:17

I adore you.
Zephaniah 3:17

So, let's not listen to any of the devil's negative lies. Let's just believe the truth of what our wonderful Savior has to say about you and me...

Believe what Jesus says about you and speak the truth out loud:

- ♥ **Jesus delights in me**
- ♥ **He rejoices over me with singing; I make His heart happy**
- ♥ **My Heavenly Father adores me**

PRAYER: *Heavenly Father, thank You so much that I don't have to be rich and famous for You to adore me; You love me right now, just the way I am. Your word says that You are pleased with me because I have put my faith in Jesus. You don't even remember my past mistakes. Thank You so much for adoring me, Lord; it makes me feel so loved!*

STUDY QUESTIONS

Have you ever heard these lies?

You **will** only be adored if
you are rich and famous   _____Yes _____ No

No one admires you   _____Yes _____ No

No one adores you   _____Yes _____ No

Why do you think people want to be admired and adored?

_____

_____

NOW LET'S STUDY THE TRUTH TOGETHER

Read **Zephaniah 3:17**: *The Lord your God is in the midst of you, a Mighty One, a Savior [Who saves]! He will rejoice over you with joy, He will rest [in silent satisfaction] and <u>in His love</u> He will be silent and make no mention [of past sins, or even recall them], He will exult over you with singing.* AMP

This verse says that Jesus doesn't even mention your mistakes. He doesn't even remember anything you've done wrong. What is Jesus doing when He looks at you?

_____

_____

Jesus is singing a love song to you. Here are some of His actual words from the Bible:

> Oh, my dear friend! You're so beautiful!
> And your eyes so beautiful—like doves!
> Let me see your face, let me hear your voice.
> For your voice is soothing and your face is ravishing
> You're so beautiful, my darling, so beautiful!
> Song of Songs 1:15, 2:14, 4:1 MSG

Wow! These are the words Jesus is actually singing to us, taken from the Song of Songs. Take time to really think about what you've read. How does it make you feel? Are you getting the idea of how much you are adored?

_____

_____

_____

Write **T** next to the statements that are true and **L** next to the ones that are lies:

_____ No one adores me

_____ No one admires me

_____ I have to be famous to be admired and adored

_____ Jesus delights in me

_____ Jesus sings over me with joy

_____ Jesus adores me

GOING DEEPER

TRUTH: Jesus adores me

Read **Jude 1:24** in your Bible.

What does this verse say that Jesus has done for you?

_____

_____

Read **Zephaniah 3:17** again.
How does it make your heart feel to realize that you are adored by your Heavenly Father?

_____

_____

_____

JOURNAL ENTRY

Write a prayer to your Heavenly Father about what you've learned today. Share your heart with Him:

_____

_____

_____

_____

_____

What is the main truth that you learned from today's devotion:

_____

_____

_____

_____

Day 3
I Am Gifted

Each of you has received a gift to use to serve others. Be good servants of God's various gifts of grace. — *1 Peter 4:10 NCV*

s I watch the *American Idol* TV show, it's easy for me to get caught up in all the glitz. I mean, who wouldn't want to wear those beautiful designer outfits, or have your face and hair made up by celebrity stylists? As I watch the singers' picture-perfect faces beaming from the TV screen, it's tempting for me to believe that singing is the only important gift. But I know better, having been involved on both sides of the stage, that it takes all kinds of talented people to put on a production; in fact, a whole group of people that no one ever sees. They are the backstage people: from the director, to the stage crew, to the band, and they work tirelessly behind the scenes making sure the show goes perfectly and the performers look great. And even though they are not seen, their gift is just as important. Without them, the show could not go on, and we would not be blessed by it.

The above scripture tells us that God has given each one of us a unique gift to use to serve and bless others, and that even though our gifts may vary, they are all equally important. But the devil would like us to think differently, so he messes with our heads. I remember as a teenager that I had a friend who seemed to be able to do everything really well. She was considered a genius. She played the piano, the guitar and the clarinet. She even taught herself how to read and write music. Not only that, she got an A+ in every subject at school, even calculus! I was also a good student, but no matter how hard I tried, I could never measure up to her.

This experience made me question myself, and the devil was right there to add fuel to the fire. He would feed these thoughts into my mind, and not knowing the truth, I would fall for his lies:

Your gift is not as good as her's
Your gift is way better than her's
Hang it up; you don't have a gift at all!

This cycle of comparison did not stop until I really began to see myself the way that God saw me; that I was loved and that God had a special plan for my life and that He had given me unique gifts for that purpose. The Good News is that as I looked to Him and began to see just how much He loved me, my gift of writing began to develop and God is now using it to serve and bless others. At the same time, He is developing His gifts in my friends, too, so there's absolutely no need to compare ourselves with each other!

Listen to the truth which Jesus speaks to you and me about our gifts…

All the gifts I give are equally important.
I Corinthians 12:7

Your gift is important.
I Peter 4:10

I have given you a special gift to bless others.
I Peter 4:10

So, agree with Jesus and watch Him develop the gifts He has placed inside you. Say these truths out loud:

- ♥ **Jesus has given everyone important and wonderful gifts**
- ♥ **My gift is important**
- ♥ **Jesus has given me a precious gift to bless others**

PRAYER: *Thank You, Lord, for giving me a very special gift. Help me to remember how unique and important it is; give me the grace not to feel like my gift is better or worse than anyone else's. Father, help me to remember that all gifts come from You for the purpose of blessing others.*

STUDY QUESTIONS

Have these thoughts ever entered your mind:

LIES EXPOSED

Your gift is **way better** than your **friend's**   _____Yes _____ No

Your **gift is** not as good as your **friend's**   _____Yes _____ No

Hang **it up** — you **don't have** a **gift** at **all!**   _____Yes _____ No

How did it make you feel when you believed these lies?

_____

_____

NOW LET'S STUDY THE TRUTH TOGETHER

Read **Ephesians 2:10:** *For we are God's masterpiece. He has created us anew in Christ Jesus, so we can do the good things he planned for us long ago.*

What are you called in this passage of scripture? For what purpose did He create you anew?

_____

_____

_____

Read **1 Peter 4:10-11:** *God has given each of you a gift from his great variety of spiritual gifts. Use them well to serve one another. Do you have the gift of speaking? Then speak as though God himself were speaking through you. Do you have the gift of helping others? Do it with all the strength and energy God supplies. Then everything you do will bring glory to God through Jesus Christ.*

1 Peter 4:11 says that when you use your gift to bless others you bring glory to God. Your gift is something that you enjoy doing. What do you enjoy doing that is a blessing to others?

_____

_____

_____

Write **T** next to the statements that are true and **L** next to the ones that are lies:

_____ My gift is important

_____ I don't have any gifts

_____ Her gift is better than mine

_____ God has given everyone a special gift

_____ The gift I have is not important

_____ God wants to help me use my gift to bless others

GOING DEEPER

TRUTH: **Jesus has given me gifts to bless others**

Read **Romans 12:4-8** in your Bible.

What are some of the gifts God gives?

_____

_____

Read **1 Corinthians 12:7:** _Each person is given something to do that shows who God is: Everyone gets in on it, everyone benefits. All kinds of things are handed out by the Spirit, and to all kinds of people! The variety is wonderful._ MSG

How do you think the gift God has given you shows Who He is?

_____

_____

_____

How does your gift benefit others?

_____

_____

_____

Fill in the blank using the Scripture from above:

God gives gifts to everyone. The variety is _____.

JOURNAL ENTRY

In your own words, write a prayer below thanking God for your specific gift, and asking Him to help you use it to bless others:

_____

_____

_____

_____

_____

What is the main truth that you learned from today's devotion?

_____

_____

_____

_____

_____

you are gifted

you are adored!

you are wonderful

147

WEEK 8

EXTREME MAKEOVER

You're Loving Because of Jesus

Rose Karlebach

Day 1
I Am Loving

Day 2
I Am Forgiving

Day 3
I Am an Encourager

Day 1
I Am Loving

May Christ through your faith [actually] dwell (settle down, abide, make His permanent home) in your hearts! May you be rooted deep in love and founded securely on love. — *Ephesians 3:17* AMP

Have you ever watched the show, *Extreme Makeover*? On it we see an old home being rebuilt brand new for a family to move into and live their life in. Were you aware that in a very real way, your heart is just like the houses on that show? The above scripture tells us that Jesus has actually made His home in you, inside your heart and that He wants to live His life through you. What's cool, is that just like on the TV show, when Jesus moves in He removes all of the old nasty junk that doesn't work well, and makes everything brand new! The old you disappears and as **2 Corinthians 5:17** says *Anyone who belongs to Christ is a new person. The past is forgotten, and everything is new.* CEV In **Ezekiel 11:19** it says something similar, *I will give them one heart [a new heart] and I will put a new spirit within them; and I will take the stony [unnaturally hardened] heart out of their flesh, and will give them a heart of flesh [sensitive and responsive to the touch of their God].* AMP Wow! Not only are you a new person, but God is giving you a brand new loving heart, sensitive and responsive to Him! This means that your very nature now, because Jesus lives inside you, is love. This means that you can live life in a new way, responding to what God says about you instead of the way you've responded in the past. Jesus makes you a brand new person, and changes the way you think.

When I was younger, I lived and worked in New York City. On one particular evening as I waited for the train to take me home, a sweet young girl came up to me and started talking to me about Jesus. Well, at the time I really didn't want to hear about Jesus, and didn't appreciate her bothering me, so in a very unkind way I basically told her to "bug off" and leave me alone. My words were so harsh that she ended up walking off the platform in hysterical tears. I responded to her in that way because that is how I saw myself, as tough and mean, which I thought I had to be to survive in that big city.

Now, anyone who saw me that day would have agreed that I was indeed a very tough and mean person because of the way they had seen me act. But the real truth was that I was not tough at all, but rather, insecure, unhappy and scared, and I acted that way because I believed the devil's lies and didn't want anyone to know how I really felt. The sad part is I didn't even realize that the poor girl was trying to give me the answer to my insecurity: Jesus! As you can imagine, later on, I felt really bad about what I had done, so the devil used his lies to make me feel even worse about myself. This is what he said to me:

You are not a loving person

You are mean and unkind

You don't even like people

Some years later, I moved out of New York City, and eventually did ask Jesus to come and live in my heart. He did an extreme makeover on my heart and made me a brand new person. Over the course of time, I began to get a very different opinion of myself based on what Jesus says about me. As I did that, the old me starting disappearing and I began acting more and more like Jesus. The more I looked to Him to help me love others with His love, the more He lived through me. Here are the words Jesus spoke to me which caused my heart to change...

As I've said, I have come to know the difference between the devil's lies and the truth of what Jesus says about me. Occasionally, however, I still make the mistake of acting in an unloving way. The nice thing is, that now when that happens, I don't have to live in condemnation. I can simply turn to Jesus and let His words remind me of who I am in Him.

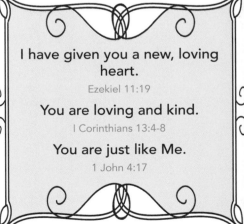

I have given you a new, loving heart.
Ezekiel 11:19

You are loving and kind.
I Corinthians 13:4-8

You are just like Me.
1 John 4:17

So, the next time the devil tries to fill your head with his lies, just tell him "Talk to the hand devil, 'cuz the heart ain't listening!" Let Jesus remind you that you are a loving and kind person because that's how He made you and He lives inside of you! So, agree with the One who loves you.

Speak the truth out loud:

- ♥ **I have a new, loving heart**
- ♥ **I am loving and kind**
- ♥ **I am just like Jesus!**

PRAYER: *Lord, thank You for coming to live in my heart and making me a brand new person. Thank You for taking away my old, hardened heart and giving me a new, loving heart that is sensitive and responsive to Your touch. Help me to always remember who You say I am. You gave me your very nature and I am loving and kind, just like You. I have Your power to love others because You first loved me.*

STUDY QUESTIONS

Have you ever fallen for any of these negative lies of the devil:

You are not a **loving person**	_____Yes	_____ No
You are **mean and unkind**	_____Yes	_____ No
You are not **like Jesus**	_____Yes	_____ No

NOW, LET'S STUDY THE TRUTH TOGETHER

Today we saw how Jesus has given you a new, loving heart, sensitive and responsive to God. Let's take a look at the qualities you have, because Jesus has made you a loving person.

Read **1 Corinthians 13:4-5, 7-8:**

> *Love endures long and is patient and kind;*
> *Love never is envious nor boils over with jealousy . . . .*
> *It is not conceited (arrogant and inflated with pride);*
> *It is not rude (unmannerly) and does not act unbecomingly.*
> *Love (God's love in us) does not insist on its own*
> *rights or seek its own way,*
> *For it is not self-seeking;*
> *it is not touchy or fretful or resentful;*
> *It takes no account of the evil done to it*
> *[it pays no attention to a suffered wrong].*
> *Is ever ready to believe the best of every person....*
> *Love never fails [never fades out or becomes obsolete*
> *or comes to an end].* AMP

Because of Jesus, this is who you really are. Now fill in the blanks below with your name and read the paragraph out loud:

_____ endures long and is patient and kind; she is never envious nor boils over with jealousy. _____ is not conceited, arrogant nor inflated with pride. She is not rude (unmannerly) and does not act unbecomingly. _____ does not insist on her own rights or seek her own way. She is not touchy, fretful or resentful. _____ takes no account of the evil done to her [pays no attention to a suffered wrong]. _____ is ever ready to believe the best of every person. [God's love in _____] [never fades out or becomes obsolete or comes to an end].

Write **T** next to the statements that are true and **L** next to the statements that are lies:

_____ I am not a loving person
_____ Jesus gave me a new heart just like His
_____ I am mean and unkind
_____ My new nature is loving and kind
_____ I am just like Jesus

GOING DEEPER

TRUTH: **Jesus gave me a loving heart**

Have you ever experienced an incident similar to the one in today's reading where the devil tried to convince you of his lies? How did it make your heart feel?

_____

_____

_____

Now tell of a time recently when you did something kind for someone. How did it make your heart feel?

_____

_____

_____

Read **Ephesians 4:22-24** and **32.**
According to verse 23, how do you put on your new nature and let Jesus love others through you?_____

_____

Read **Ezekiel 36:26-27.**

What does verse 26 tell you God will do for you?

_____

What does verse 27 say God will put within you?

_____

What will that enable you to do according to these verses?

_____

JOURNAL ENTRY

Now write a prayer to Jesus, thanking Him for your new, loving nature:

_____

_____

_____

_____

_____

What is the main truth that you have learned from today's devotion?

_____

_____

_____

_____

_____

❧

Day 2
I Am Forgiving

*Take on an entirely new way of life—a God-fashioned life, a life
renewed from the inside and working itself into your conduct as God
accurately reproduces his character in you.* — Ephesians 4:24 MSG

y husband and I used to live in NYC, where his company took old
buildings, fixed them up inside and made them brand new. You learned
in our last devotional that Jesus did the same kind of *Extreme Makeover*
inside of you, making you new from the inside out. The above scripture
tells us to **take on a new way of life**, a life fashioned by God, in which
He works His very nature into our character. This happens as we look to
Him and take on His opinion of ourselves. **1 Corinthians 13:5** describes
the difference between the "old" us and the "new." It says that we are no
longer **touchy or fretful or resentful,** like we used to be, and we **take. . .
no account of the evil done to** us and we **pay. . . no attention to a suffered
wrong.** AMP Because you have Jesus' very nature inside of you, as you look
to Him for strength, He helps you to forgive those who do you wrong.

During high school, my slightly younger sister and I both had part-time
jobs, and we would each buy our own clothing. We rarely shared clothes
as we were different sizes. Waking up late one morning, I rushed to put
on the brand new outfit I had just bought: a beautiful multi-colored, tie-
dyed shirt; awesome 4-inch platform shoes and a very expensive pair
of stone-washed, low-rider, bell-bottomed jeans! Woo hoo! Would I be
looking good! But what I didn't realize was that my sneaky sister (who
could sew) had worn my new jeans the day before, and had taken them
in to fit her smaller hips! As I struggled in vain to put them on, not only
didn't they fit, but they had already been worn, and there was no time to
take out the seams. Fuming, I ended up going to school in some crummy
old mismatched outfit I threw together at the last minute as I rushed out
the door!

Later on that day when I confronted my sister, she just brushed the whole incident off as if it were no big deal, and told me to get over it! As you can imagine, I got mad and yelled at her and said some really mean things to her. Of course, the devil was right there speaking his lies to my heart. Have you ever heard these lies when you were angry about the way someone treated you:

They don't deserve to be forgiven

If you forgive them, they'll just hurt you again

It's too hard to forgive

For a long time, my sister and I did not get along because we both fell for the devil's lies. Thank goodness Jesus gave me the power to forgive her and we now have a wonderful relationship. We talk on the phone and share our hearts often, even though we live pretty far apart. Knowing what Jesus has done for me and how He has forgiven me of all my mistakes, gives me the power to forgive others who have done me wrong.

I used to be the kind of person who was touchy, fretful and resentful and held grudges against people who wronged me. I was afraid to forgive because I didn't want people to hurt me again, and I didn't want them to get away with hurting me, either. Even when I did try, it seemed the more I tried, the less I was able to forgive. I struggled with this for years.

The problem is, if you follow this kind of faulty thinking it makes it harder and harder to have any friends, because eventually, everyone you know will have an opportunity to hurt or offend you! It's a lose/lose situation and does not make for good relationships.

But that is exactly what I love about Jesus. He is the answer to every kind of relationship problem we may face. As I looked to Him and studied His word, I began to realize how much He loved me, and because He gave me his righteousness, I already had his loving, forgiving nature in my heart. I stopped listening to the devil and began to listen to the truth that Jesus speaks to my heart.

This is what He says to you and me....

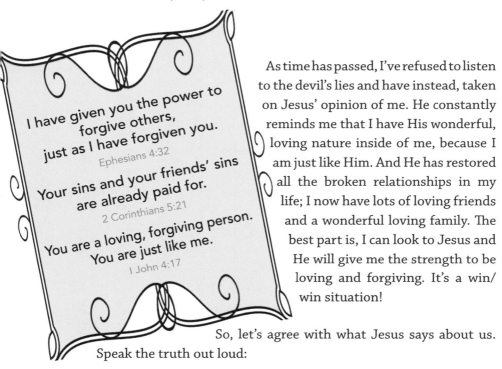

I have given you the power to forgive others, just as I have forgiven you.

Ephesians 4:32

Your sins and your friends' sins are already paid for.

2 Corinthians 5:21

You are a loving, forgiving person. You are just like me.

I John 4:17

As time has passed, I've refused to listen to the devil's lies and have instead, taken on Jesus' opinion of me. He constantly reminds me that I have His wonderful, loving nature inside of me, because I am just like Him. And He has restored all the broken relationships in my life; I now have lots of loving friends and a wonderful loving family. The best part is, I can look to Jesus and He will give me the strength to be loving and forgiving. It's a win/win situation!

So, let's agree with what Jesus says about us. Speak the truth out loud:

- ♥ Jesus gives me the power to forgive others just as He has forgiven me

- ♥ My sins and everyone else's sins have been paid for

- ♥ I am a loving, forgiving person; I am just like Jesus

PRAYER: *Heavenly Father, help me to forgive those who have done me wrong. I don't want to believe the devil's lies and live a life of broken relationships. Thank you for giving me a new nature that is just like Jesus and giving me a loving and forgiving heart. Thank You for giving me the power to forgive others just as You have forgiven me.*

STUDY QUESTIONS

Have you ever heard these negative thoughts:

LIES EXPOSED

They don't **deserve** to be **for**given	_____Yes	_____ No
If you for**give** them, they'll just **hur**t you again	_____Yes	_____ No
It's too **hard** to for**give**	_____Yes	_____ No

NOW LET'S STUDY THE TRUTH TOGETHER

1 John 4:17 says that as Jesus is *so are we in this world.* That means you have a heart just like Jesus.

Read **Ephesians 4:32:** *Be kind and compassionate to one another, for-giving each other, just as in Christ God forgave you.* NIV

You are just like Jesus. What does this verse say about your new nature?

_____

_____

Read **1 Corinthians 13:5:** It says that your new nature of love, *is not touchy or fretful or resentful; it takes no account of the evil done to it [it pays no attention to a suffered wrong].* AMP

Insert your name in the following sentences:

_____ **is not touchy, fretful, or resentful**

_____ **does not take account of the evil done to her**

_____ **pays no attention to a suffered wrong**

Write **T** next to the statements that are true and **L** next to the statements that are lies:

_____ It's too hard to forgive

_____ They don't deserve to be forgiven

_____ You should be afraid of being hurt again

_____ Jesus has given me a new, forgiving nature

_____ Jesus gives me the power to forgive those who do me wrong

_____ I am just like Jesus

GOING DEEPER

TRUTH: **Jesus gives me the power to forgive**

Have you ever had someone treat you badly and you struggled to forgive them? Explain: _____

_____

_____

What negative thoughts was the devil putting in your mind during this time? _____

_____

_____

Read **Philippians 2:13** in your Bible.

Do you have to depend on your own strength to forgive? What does this verse say Jesus will do in you when you ask Him?

_____

_____

Read **Hebrews 4:16.** What does this verse say God will do for you if you're having a challenge forgiving someone?

_____

_____

In whose strength, then, do you forgive?

_____

_____

JOURNAL ENTRY

Now that you know that Jesus will help you forgive, write a prayer thanking Him for your new forgiving nature, and asking Him to help you forgive those who have hurt you:

_____

_____

_____

_____

_____

What is the main truth that you learned from today's devotion?

_____

_____

_____

_____

Day 3
I Am an Encourager

Let everything you say be good and helpful, so that your words will be an encouragement to those who hear them.

— Ephesians 4:29 NLT

On *Extreme Makeover,* each week we watch as a house is rebuilt on the inside. You've learned this week that Jesus rebuilt you and made His home in your heart. He encourages you with His words of love, reminding you of who you are in Him. When you keep your thoughts on His words of encouragement toward you, words of encouragement effortlessly flow out of you towards others. It's part of your new nature of love. You are just like Jesus. By speaking words of love and encouragement, you help "build your friends up," inside. **Ephesians 4:29** encourages you to speak words that will help others become stronger, and do them good. The Message Bible says it in this way, *Say only what helps, each word a gift.* 1 Thessalonians 5:11 goes on to say, *Encourage each other and build each other up.* *Encourage* means "to inspire with courage, spirit, or confidence." [19]

Proverbs 18:21 says, *What you say can mean life or death.* NCV I did not grow up realizing the power of my words and their effect on others. If I felt like saying something, I would just say it without even thinking. One incident I remember involved my mother, who had just bought a beautiful gold gown to go to a special dinner party with my dad. Being the eldest child, she asked me how I thought she looked. Well, I was upset with her over something, so I told her that she looked ugly! My poor, precious mom ran out of the room in tears, and I felt terrible for being so thoughtless! But it was too late, the damage had been done.

For a long time, I was plagued with guilty thoughts, because I believed I had damaged my mother's heart, and could not be forgiven. The devil used this incident to fill my head with his lies. This is what he said to me:

You are bad; your words hurt people

You can never be forgiven

You have damaged her heart

Well, thank God for Jesus! Because He paid for all our sins, even when we do make a huge blunder with our words, we are forgiven and it's just as if it never happened! And He is so willing to heal our heart and the heart of the person we've hurt.

I did later go back to my mom and ask her to forgive me (which of course she did, being the wonderful mom she is!) What's interesting is, when I brought it up, she said to me, "Well, to tell you the truth, I didn't even remember it!" I had been so concerned, and yet, because Jesus is so wonderful, He had already erased it from her memory and healed her heart too! He released me from my mistake and gave me a fresh start. I am free to be an encourager, and it's all because of Jesus!

Jesus empowers us to speak words of encouragement and love to the people we care about, as we look to Him for his grace. These are His words of truth that so encouraged my heart…

Wow! What a relief! Jesus has healed my heart, helping me to forget my past mistakes and giving me the ability and grace to speak words of life to people. I am no longer plagued by the enemy's lies, but actually love being an encourager, and using my words as gifts to build my friends and family up! I love the fact that my words really are a gift, more precious than anything else I could give to those I love.

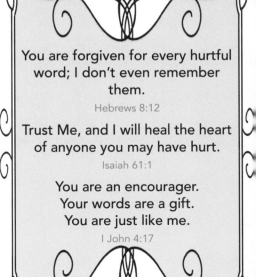

You are forgiven for every hurtful word; I don't even remember them.

Hebrews 8:12

Trust Me, and I will heal the heart of anyone you may have hurt.

Isaiah 61:1

You are an encourager.
Your words are a gift.
You are just like me.

I John 4:17

Not too long ago, my mom – who hadn't even finished high school when I was growing up – graduated from a major university and received her college degree. During the years that led up to her graduation, we would often talk on the phone and I would encourage her in her pursuit of her education, by saying, "That's great! You can do it, Mom!" and, "Wow! You are amazing!" I wanted my words to help her to keep on going because she was not only working full time during the day, but also leading Bible Studies in the evenings.

As she walked off the stage that special day, diploma in hand and a great big grin across her face, my heart swelled with love and respect for her. I couldn't stop myself from giving her a huge hug and saying, "Mom, I'm so very proud of you!" and I really meant it because I knew how important this accomplishment was to her and how hard she had worked to achieve it. I wanted her to hear how I felt, with my words.

Just like me, you too, are an encourager because of Jesus, so agree with what He says about you:

- **I am forgiven for every hurtful word I've ever spoken**

- **Jesus will heal the heart of anyone I may have hurt**

- **I am an encourager, my words are a gift; I am just like Jesus**

PRAYER: *Thank You, Lord, that You have made me an encourager and that the words I speak are a gift to the people I care about. Help me to turn to You for strength when I'm tempted to say something unkind. Thank You for forgiving me of all the times I've said hurtful things. You don't even remember any negative word I've ever said. If I've hurt someone in any way, please heal their heart. Give me the courage to go to them and work it out, or apologize. Help me to speak words that will help others become strong, and only do them good! Thank You for making me just like You!*

STUDY QUESTIONS

Have these condemning thoughts ever gone through your mind:

LIES EXPOSED

You are bad;
your words hurt people   _____Yes   _____ No

You can never be forgiven   _____Yes   _____ No

You should be ashamed
of yourself   _____Yes   _____ No

Have you ever said anything to someone that you regretted later on? How did that make you feel?

_____

_____

_____

NOW LET'S STUDY THE TRUTH TOGETHER

Read **Hebrews 8:12**, God says: *"I will forgive their wrongdoings, and I will never again remember their sins."* NLT

According to the above scripture, what two things has Jesus done about the hurtful words you may have spoken?

1. _____   2. _____

Read **1 Thessalonians 5:11**: *Encourage each other and build each other up.*

Write down something encouraging you said to someone recently:

_____

_____

_____

_____

_____

See, you are an encourager!

Write **T** next to the statements that are true and **L** next to the ones that are lies:

_____ I am bad because I've spoken unkind words to people

_____ When I make a mistake, Jesus forgives me and forgets all the bad things I've said

_____ Jesus will empower me to speak encouraging words

_____ My words are not a gift

_____ I am an encourager; I am just like Jesus

GOING DEEPER

TRUTH: **I am an encourager; I am just like Jesus**

Look up and read **Ephesians 4:29** in your own Bible.

Now, read the same scripture from the Message Bible: *Say only what helps, each word a gift.*

Now, describe what these two passages say about you:

_____

_____

Read **Proverbs 18:21** in your own Bible.

What does this verse say about the power of your words?

_____

Every time you listen to Jesus' words of love toward you it brings life to your heart. But when you listen to the devil's lies it brings death to your heart. There is life in Jesus' words and death in the devil's words.

Throughout this whole Bible study you have been listening to the loving, encouraging words that Jesus speaks to your heart. He has told you the Good News that you are royalty, and a genuine princess in His kingdom. You are loved, righteous, wise, beautiful, valuable, accepted, wonderful and loving because Jesus lives inside of you. As you daily remember what

He says about you and live in His love, you'll be empowered to share this same Good News with your family and friends. You'll build others up and bring life to those around you. Remember, you are just like Jesus and each word you speak is a gift.

JOURNAL ENTRY

Write down a prayer, asking Jesus to help you encourage others with words of love:

_____

_____

_____

_____

_____

What is the main truth that you learned from today's devotion?

_____

_____

_____

_____

_____

"Talk to the hand devil, 'cuz the heart ain't listening!"

"I believe what Jesus says about me!"

REFERENCES

WEEK 1 TRADING PLACES

Day 2 I Am Righteous

1 *Righteous*: Romans 5:8-9 AMP; 2 Timothy 2:22 AMP, Deuteronomy 6:25 AMP; *Lexical Aids of the New Testament. http://dictionary.reference.com/browse/ righteous*

WEEK 3 ARE YOU SMARTER THAN A FIFTH GRADER?

Day 3 I Am Confident

2 *Confidence: http://www.lexipedia.com/english/confidence.*
3 *Self-confidence: www.dictionary.reference.com,* definition 2 of "self-confidence; *http://lexipedia.com/english/self-confidence.*

WEEK 4 AMERICA'S NEXT TOP MODEL

Day 1 I Am Beautiful

4 *Glory: 1.doxa, Strong's 1391. Vine's Complete Expository Dictionary of Old and New Testament Words* © 1984, 1996, Thomas Nelson, Inc., Nashville, TN.
5 *Beautiful;* World Book Dictionary, Vol. 1 (online).
6 *Beautiful: Yapha, http://strongsnumbers.com/hebrew/3313.htm.*

Day 3 I Am Beautiful Within

7 Whitney Thomas, *America's Next Top Model*
8 Jaslene, *America's Next Top Model*

WEEK 5 THE COMPARISON TRAP

Day 1 I Am Valuable

9 Synonyms for *valuable:* "Webster's New World Thesaurus ™", Third Edition, © 1997.

Day 3 I Am Worthy of Love

10 Expression: *"apple of God's eye,"* see Zechariah 2:8 *www.biblegateway.com/ resources/commentaries/Matthew-Henry/Zech/Jews-Called-Return-Own-Land*

Day 4 I Am Worth the Wait

11 *Justified; justification: http://dictionary.reference.com/browse/justification.*

WEEK 6 BEST FRIENDS FOREVER

Day 1 I Am Accepted

12 Synonyms for *accepted:* Webster's New World Thesaurus™, Third Edition, © 1997.

Day 2 I Am Approved

13 Definition and synonyms of *approve: http://dictionary.reference.com/browse/approve.*

Day 3 I Am Favored

14 *Favor: http://dictionary.reference.com/browse/favor.*

WEEK 7 AMERICAN IDOL

Day 1 I Am Wonderful

15 Definition and synonyms of *wonderful: http://dictionary.reference.com/browse/wonderful.*
16 *Awful: http://dictionary.reference.com/browse/awful.*

Day 2 I Am Adored

17 *Adore: http://dictionary.reference.com/browse/adore.*
18 *Exult: http://dictionary.reference.com/browse/exult.*

WEEK 8 EXTREME MAKEOVER

Day 3 I Am An Encourager

19 *Encourage: http://dictionary.reference.com/browse/encourage.*

CONNIE WITTER is a speaker, author, and Bible study teacher. Her best selling book, *P.S. God Loves You*, has sold over 150,000 copies. She is the founder of Because of Jesus Ministries which was established in 2006.

She has been teaching ladies Bible studies for 15 years. Her Bible study *Because of Jesus* was published in 2002 which is the foundation of her life and ministry. Since 2005, she has held an annual *Because of Jesus Women's Conference* in Tulsa, Oklahoma.

Connie has traveled throughout the United States and Russia sharing the life-changing message of *Because of Jesus*. She has been the guest speaker at Women's Conferences, ladies retreats, ladies meetings, and has also spoken into the lives of teenage girls. She has been a guest on several Christian TV programs. Her weekly TV program, *Because of Jesus* can be seen world wide through her ministry website, *becauseofJesus.com*. Each week she shares the Good News that we are righteous, valuable, precious, blameless, blessed, favored and extravagantly loved by God because of Jesus. Thousands of lives have been changed through her ministry.

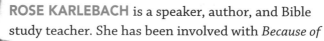

ROSE KARLEBACH is a speaker, author, and Bible study teacher. She has been involved with *Because of Jesus Ministries* for many years and has been a featured speaker at the *Because of Jesus Women's Conferences*. She has been the guest speaker at ladies retreats and meetings. She has taught several Bible Studies, including her favorite, the *Song of Jesus*. She uses practical insight and humor to reveal God's unconditional love and grace in a life-changing way.

KELLY RAY has been involved in supportive roles in ministry for 15 years. She facilitated in groups such as *Beginning Again* divorce recovery group, *Victory by Virtue* through Victory Christian Center and most recently with *Because of Jesus Ministries*. She has helped with *Because of Jesus Conferences* and was a workshop speaker at the 2007 Conference. She has led young girl's Bible study groups. She is a gifted writer and speaker who is passionate about teaching young girls the truth of who they are in Jesus so they will know how much their Heavenly Father loves them.

OTHER BOOKS BY CONNIE WITTER

Because of Jesus Bible Study

P.S. God Loves You

21 Days to Discover Who You Are in Jesus

We would love to hear how this Bible Study/Devotional
has impacted your life.
To contact the authors write:

P.O. Box 3064
Broken Arrow, OK 74013
Contact@becauseofJesus.com

For additional copies of this book go to:
becauseofJesusbookstore.com
Or call
918-994-6500